HOW TO JUMP-START YOUR UNION

HOW TO JUMP-START YOUR UNION

Lessons from the Chicago Teachers

Alexandra Bradbury
Mark Brenner
Jenny Brown
Jane Slaughter
Samantha Winslow

A LABOR NOTES BOOK

A LABOR NOTES BOOK

Copyright © 2014 by Labor Education and Research Project

First printing: January 2014
Second printing: October 2015

About the Publisher

Labor Notes is a media and organizing project that since 1979 has been the voice of union activists who want to put the movement back in the labor movement. Through its magazine, website, books, schools, and conferences, Labor Notes brings together a network of members and leaders who know the labor movement is worth fighting for. Visit our website at www.labornotes.org.

Reprints

Permission is granted to workplace activists, unions, rank-and-file union groups and labor studies programs to reprint sections of this book for free distribution. Please let Labor Notes know of such use, at editor@labornotes.org, 718-284-4144, or the addresses below. Requests for permission to reprint for other purposes should be directed to Labor Notes.

Labor Notes
7435 Michigan Ave.
Detroit, MI 48210

Labor Notes
104 Montgomery St.
Brooklyn, NY 11225

Cover design: Stacey Luce
Inside design: Jenny Brown

Cover photo:
Tannen Maury ©2012 European Pressphoto Agency / Alamy

Printed in Canada

ISBN-13: 978-0-914093-01-5

Dedicated to Chicago's students, to the educators who are teaching them a better world is possible, and to the readers who will learn from CTU's example and go out to start their own fires.

Contents

Allying with other groups for militant rallies. Action changes the conversation again: not a longer school day but a better school day. Fighting school closings. Confrontational tactics. Making a positive proposal: "The Schools Chicago's Students Deserve."

Foreword

Chicago Teachers Show How It's Done

by Jen Johnson

I became an activist when I was teaching history at Lincoln Park High and my principal started firing union delegates.

First, my mentor teacher was let go; then my union mentor, our librarian. I was untenured and scared and just being ushered into union work. After these losses I needed to do more, learn more, and shake off my fears.

Luckily, I joined a small group of idealistic educators—veteran teachers and new unionists—to form CORE, the Caucus of Rank-and-File Educators, in 2008. We set out on a mission to defend public education in Chicago. We built a caucus that would win leadership of the Chicago Teachers Union in 2010 and lead its first strike in 25 years.

How did we get to the point of going out on a nine-day strike? Why are the battle lines drawn so clearly in Chicago when it comes to public schools?

The labor movement has always been "about inspiration and struggle, about ordinary people transforming the world—and themselves in the process," as unionist Joe Burns wrote in his 2011 book *Reviving the Strike*. But our union had fallen into the same trap as most labor organizations in the last few decades: compromise and collaboration with management. Our union had protected basic job security and continued the flow of modest raises—but we hadn't done enough to oppose the destruction of public schools.

Our children's schools were being closed. Our members were losing their jobs. Union-busting had come to dominate the national and local dialogue about education reform, with a single-minded focus on teacher quality and standardized tests. The voices of experienced educators were being lost.

Though our union leaders did speak against closing schools and replacing them with charters, the full power of the membership was never brought to bear. Instead of talking about what is best for kids, our union to some degree accepted the premise that poor-quality teachers were the main problem.

"We know collaboration works," our former union president said in a 2009 address to the City Club of Chicago—whose members were behind destructive policies like the blitz of school closures. The union agreed to experiments in merit pay.

When CORE took on the job of leading the CTU in 2010, we took on the task of becoming the leading institution of the movement for education justice. The union had to change the public debate, bringing in the voices of its 27,000 members.

Mayor Rahm Emanuel and his corporate friends had created the perfect formula to bring on a teachers' strike—by raking teachers over the coals and driving them out of a profession they loved; by closing schools year after year, replacing them with non-union charters that kicked kids out left and right; by shuffling students around the city in the midst of poverty and violence;

Jen Johnson

by adding days to the school calendar for more standardized testing instead of richer instruction; and finally, by telling teachers they would have to work as many as six more weeks with no more pay.

After all that, members were not prepared to just shut up. When we voted to strike, we took back our power as a union. We said we weren't scared any more.

Our allies saw that we weren't just fighting for pay increases. We were determined to change the discussion about public education to focus on our students. At the height of the strike, a poll found that a majority of the city and 66 percent of parents of Chicago Public Schools students supported us over the mayor. The numbers were even higher among blacks and Latinos than among whites.

The strike did not achieve all the educational goals laid out in our manifesto, *The Schools Chicago's Students Deserve*, but it did wake up the city—and the nation—to some of our truths. The dialogue about public education can no longer simply assume that teachers are the problem, that no other issues exist. Parents will not be passive actors when it comes to policies that affect their children. And we showed that teachers unions are not merely protectionist organizations but can be a progressive force for education justice.

A recent Hechinger Education Report says teacher job satisfaction is at a 25-year low. We believe this malaise can be converted into action. After CTU members walked the picket line, we saw a wave of teacher strikes in Illinois. We are witnessing the awakening of teachers unions across the country.

We are still under violent attack in Chicago, with nearly 50 schools closed in 2013. As the closings were announced, thousands of parents, students, teachers, and community members packed hearings to passionately defend their schools. Students are starting their own organizations and taking action.

The strike was not built overnight, and it did not magically build the schools we teachers all want to work in. But it proved that we can fight harder, smarter—and win.

Jen Johnson was a classroom teacher for 10 years. She now works for CTU on teacher evaluation.

1

Why This Book—And How to Use It

The sight of tens of thousands of striking teachers and their allies marching through the streets of Chicago was a much-needed shot in the arm for a sagging labor movement.

For more than a week in September 2012, the Chicago Teachers Union went toe to toe with Mayor Rahm Emanuel and the city's political and financial elites—fighting them to a draw at the bargaining table and besting them handily in the battle for the city's hearts and minds.

It's all too easy to lapse into pessimism about what workers are capable of, whether unions still have power, whether strikes are still viable. But in perhaps the most impressive strike since the UPS walkout in 1997, Chicago's educators demonstrated that the strike is still labor's most powerful weapon.

In the process, CTU upended the conventional wisdom that public employees and taxpayers are inevitably at odds. For both groups, the real enemy is the 1%. The teachers branded Chicago's public schools an example of "educational apartheid" and talked openly about the racial inequalities built into the mayor's plan—proving that unions can tackle thorny social issues head on and still win support from both members and the public.

A Different Kind of Union

Just as important, the CTU experience shows how a run-of-the-mill, bureaucratic union can be transformed with the right combination of rank-and-file organizing, hard work, and trust in democracy.

CTU's leaders took office in 2010, swept into power by an energetic reform movement, the Caucus of Rank-and-File Educators. Reform caucuses, once in office, too often start to look like their predecessors. But CORE had laid a firmer foundation than most.

For years before they were elected, CORE activists had led by example—organizing teachers to fight school closings, pushing back on punitive policies, and working side by side with parents and community organizations.

This book tells how these activists transformed their union from the bottom up, and built to a strike that was about more than bread and butter.

A How-To Handbook

We believe *How to Jump-Start Your Union*'s greatest value is as a handbook. Using the same style that has made our *Trouble-maker's Handbooks* a resource for activists, we show "how they did it" so that anyone can figure out "how to do it" in their own union and workplace.

We spell out CTU's organizing model, on tasks ranging from talking to your co-workers to building lasting community alliances to carrying out a strike vote, and much more. Those who want to run a caucus or a contract campaign will find out how here.

Before we dive into the CTU story, in Chapter 2 we set the stage by describing the damage the forces of corporate education reform had done to Chicago's schools. The "how to" chapters begin with 3 and 4, which show how the CORE caucus was forged in battles against school closures, and how it ran for office and won.

Sarah Jane Rhee, loveandstrugglephotos.com

Chapter 5 details the painstaking work of building the union back up at the grassroots, in each school: how the union reorganized itself internally to get more members into action. Chapter 6 describes working with community organizations, and Chapter 7 tells the lessons learned from fighting on many fronts at once in the two years before the strike. In these fights the union turned the attacks on teachers back onto the 1%.

Chapter 8 describes the year-long contract campaign that preceded the strike, including the strike vote and practice strike vote, and Chapter 9 shows the astonishing self-organization that members and parents carried on during the strike itself.

Chapter 10 tells what CTU gained and lost in the contract. Chapter 11 describes how CTU ran with its victory to keep momentum in the year after the strike. Chapter 12 sums up the lessons of the whole experience.

See the Glossary and the Timeline if you see an unfamiliar term or need help on the chronology—CTU really was fighting many battles at the same time. And read the Appendix on the national landscape of "education reform" if you want to understand why billionaires and politicians are so keen to attack educators.

We've also recapped essential lessons at the end of each chapter, so look for highlights there.

2

What They Were Up Against

The Chicago teachers' victorious strike is all the more impressive when measured against the mountain of criticism heaped on unionized public employees in recent years—and the aggressive national effort, funded by billionaires and lauded in the media, to make over the public schools.

From Washington to Hollywood, teachers and their unions have been painted as the primary culprits to blame for the problems in our public schools. Self-styled education "reformers" are pushing privately run charter schools and are determined to undermine teachers unions if they stand in the way.

In the past three years teachers have seen more far-reaching changes to their working conditions and public standing than in the previous three decades. Since 2010, teachers in many states have weathered assaults on the fundamentals of their work. These include eliminating or weakening job security, commonly known as "tenure"; tying teachers' evaluations to student performance on standardized tests; and instituting merit pay, also often linked to student test scores.

Teachers unions have, until recently, responded hesitantly and inconsistently.

It was precisely because CTU tacked in a different direction from most public sector unions and its own national union that Chicago's education workers were better able to defend themselves *and* win public support to their cause.

For a detailed analysis of the national assault on schools and teachers, see the Appendix.

Ground Zero for the Corporate Agenda

The "Chief Executive Officer" of Chicago schools from 2001 to 2009 was Arne Duncan, a former professional basketball player. Early on Duncan had built his credentials as an education reformer in the corporate mold. In 1996 he launched a charter school whose theme was to teach students financial management skills. He enthusiastically embraced the competition among schools enforced by George Bush's No Child Left Behind program, begun in 2001.

Thanks to earlier moves by Chicago Mayor Richard M. Daley and the Illinois legislature, when Duncan became schools CEO he had great latitude to implement his agenda.

In 1995 the Illinois legislature had passed a law that singled out Chicago: in school districts serving more than 500,000 residents, the elected school board would be abolished. Instead, the mayor would appoint the board. "So they're bankers, businesspeople...they don't have children in the public schools," CTU President Karen Lewis would explain later.

The law also said the Chicago district was no longer required to bargain with the union over class size, restructuring, or creation of new charters.

For the most part, CTU was caught flat-footed. A reform effort won leadership of the union in 2001 but was able to hang on for only one term. Then, starting in 2004, Daley and Duncan inflicted on Chicago the "Renaissance 2010" plan, a program for scores of school closings and "turnarounds," where a school's whole staff is fired and must reapply for their jobs.

Renaissance 2010 shuttered unionized public schools on the grounds that they had failed, and opened non-union charters with public funds. Between 2001 and 2010, 70 Chicago public schools were closed and 6,000 union jobs evaporated.

In 2009 President Barack Obama named Duncan his Secretary of Education. It was a strong signal that showed where the president and the Democratic establishment stood. And two years later, when Obama's chief of staff Rahm Emanuel ran for mayor of Chicago, he brought the same anti-teacher politics back home with him.

During his mayoral campaign, Emanuel toured a Southwest Side charter school with the chain's CEO, Juan Rangel, and declared it an "incredible success" because of its 8 a.m. to 5 p.m. day. To hammer out his education platform, he met with Rangel, Hyatt hotels billionaire Penny Pritzker, and private equity moguls Bruce Rauner and Brian Simmons. Emanuel made a longer school day and school year a centerpiece of his platform—and immediately after winning office in February 2011 he zeroed in on Chicago's schools and CTU.

Educational Apartheid

Many teachers were appalled by the city's enthusiastic push to slash resources and close schools. They knew the charters that replaced closed public schools were kicking out students who had low academic performance, disabilities, or disciplinary records, or whose first language was not English.

And they knew racism fed into the decisions on which schools to close. Those slated for closure and turnaround were nearly all in low-income black and Latino neighborhoods. "Those of us who taught in these low-income African American schools felt like our schools were targeted," said Carol Caref, a math teacher who would later direct CTU's research department. "Our kids had issues they needed help with—and instead of CPS supporting us and doing what was needed for the kids, they undermined us, like cutting back on vocational programs at my school."

Charters and selective-enrollment schools (elite high schools, where students compete for admission) were preserved and promoted. After CORE was elected CTU would publicly denounce the school board's policies as "educational apartheid."

Enrollments were in fact going down in some poor neighborhoods because families were being kicked out of public housing and scattered to other neighborhoods, as real estate developers pushed in. In fact, Renaissance 2010 targeted many of the same areas as the sweeping "Plan for Transformation"—another Mayor Daley scheme that was demolishing public housing to make way for private, "mixed-income" developments, forcing residents to move out in search of landlords who would accept housing vouchers.

As soon as school enrollment dropped, finally allowing for optimal class sizes, CPS would pull teachers out. "We were like, please keep teachers in the building!" said Caref. "We need more adults in the building!"

Duncan's slash-and-burn approach, together with CTU's tepid response, spurred teacher activists to form the Caucus of Rank-and-File Educators and push to take over the union.

By the Numbers

Educators

CTU is the third-largest teachers local in the U.S. Its 27,542 members, as of November 2013, included:

- 5,380 high school teachers
- 13,710 elementary teachers
- 3,066 paraprofessionals (including teacher assistants, school clerks, and many others)
- 162 school nurses
- 267 speech pathologists
- 866 clinicians (such as social workers, occupational therapists, physical therapists, and school psychologists)
- 3,826 retirees.

According to district figures, 25 percent of Chicago teachers were African American, 18 percent were Hispanic, 49 percent were white, and 3 percent were Asian/Hawaiian/Pacific Islander, as of January 2012.

Students

The Chicago Public Schools enrolled 404,151 students as of January 2012. Forty-two percent were African American, 44 percent Latino, 9 percent white, and 3 percent Asian/Pacific Islander.

Eighty-seven percent were from low-income families, and 12 percent had limited English proficiency. ✿

3

Rank and Filers Start Doing the Union's Job

Despite losing nearly 20 percent of the union's members to the Renaissance 2010 scheme, CTU's old guard leaders never had a plan—or the spirit—to fight the closings.

"There were all these attacks on the schools, and the union was basically silent," said math teacher Carol Caref. She joined a union committee on Renaissance 2010, but it didn't go anywhere.

When Englewood High was on the chopping block, history teacher Jackson Potter and other teachers and parents organized to stop the closure. But instead of pitching in, union higher-ups told Potter he should look for another job—and when he and other activists raised their voices in hearings, they were hushed by union officials.

Finding the union unhelpful, activist teachers began looking elsewhere for allies. They found each other—and like-minded community activists—and began to work together. The group that coalesced over a period of several years would become the Caucus of Rank-and-File Educators (CORE).

It wasn't initially about running for union office; it was about saving their schools. But the alliances established in these early fights would support CORE members through their 2010 election, the 2012 strike, and beyond.

The teacher activists and the community activists agreed that racism and gentrification were behind the closings. The teachers "were willing to partner with neighborhood folks because that's who they had the most in common with," said education organizer Jitu Brown of the Kenwood Oakland Community Organization (KOCO), an early ally in these fights.

Saving Bronzeville Schools

It was KOCO activists who led the first major fight against Renaissance 2010—and their success led teachers to seek them out for advice. The city moved in summer 2004 to implement the program's first phase, the Mid-South Plan, which proposed shutting down 20 out of 22 schools in the historically black Mid-South (Bronzeville) section of the city. (Kenwood and Oakland are neighborhoods in the Bronzeville area.)

KOCO organized a coalition of community members, Local School Councils, and activist teachers. (Local School Councils, or LSCs, existed in each Chicago school, composed of two teacher reps, six parents, two community reps, and the principal, plus a student rep in high schools. The councils have the final say on the school's budget and on hiring of the principal.) Together, this coalition was able to ward off the initial round of closures by packing city meetings, pressuring the district's alderwoman, and marching on the school board president.

But the Bronzeville schools weren't the only ones on the chopping block, and KOCO's organizing know-how was immediately in demand. Brown soon met Jesse Sharkey (who later became CTU's vice president), a history teacher on the North Side fighting the conversion of Senn High School into a military academy. They talked through the organizing strategies KOCO had used to halt the Mid-South Plan.

A Neighborhood Worth Preserving

Bronzeville, on the south shore of Lake Michigan, was once known as "Black Metropolis" and a national hub of African American culture. Sam Cooke, Louis Armstrong, and Muhammad Ali all lived there. But as industry fled Chicago in the 1970s and '80s, the area lost much of its population and plunged into poverty. Now professionals are moving in, and working-class residents are worried about being priced out. University of Illinois at Chicago professor Rico Gutstein called Bronzeville "one of the most gentrified communities in Chicago." (Even the Obama family lives nearby, at the cusp between Kenwood and Hyde Park.)

According to Jitu Brown, the Mid-South Plan was a calculated attempt to destabilize the neighborhood's working class black population and replace local black schools—despite their more than adequate performance—with selective charters that would cater to the young professionals, many also African American, who were moving into the neighborhood. ○

Brown also began to work with Potter, who later became CTU's staff coordinator, and Michael Brunson, who was then teaching at a school in the country's oldest public housing project, on the South Side, and later became recording secretary.

Potter was a young history teacher and debate team coach in a low-income black neighborhood on the South Side when in 2005 CPS announced plans to phase out Englewood High. He quickly became a leader in the fight to save the school, working closely with Brown and KOCO to organize student walkouts.

Potter also met high school teacher Xian Barrett, and the two began meeting with their students to collaborate. "My students at Julian High School got really into the Englewood fight," Barrett said, "because we could see the writing on the wall that we were the type of school that would be targeted next."

Not all these struggles produced wins as in Bronzeville. Englewood did eventually close, replaced by two new schools, one a charter. The naval academy did take over a wing of Senn High. And 2004-05 was only the first volley in the coming war over mass school closures. But that was all the more reason the growing relationships and organizing skills would be crucial.

Potter also served on the board of the Pilsen Alliance, which had formed in 1998 to defend Pilsen, a working class Mexican-American neighborhood on the Southwest Side, against an onslaught from developers. The city was taking tax dollars that should have gone to schools and funneling them to developers through "tax-increment financing" (TIF).

On paper the subsidies were supposed to promote job-creating industrial development in Pilsen—but there was nothing to stop the money from flowing to new condos and big-box retailers instead. The Pilsen Alliance organized against TIF financing for Target and other big-box stores, bringing Potter into coalitions with community organizations like the Grassroots Collaborative and ACORN.

'Who Wants to Talk?'

Over the next couple of years, as teachers and community activists fought side by side to save schools, the union's leaders continued to be unsupportive. Activists pushed them to create a union committee to counter Renaissance 2010. "We cajoled them

for a couple months," said Potter, and "they said yes. We got good at putting demands on union leadership together with community groups." But in spring 2007 the union dismantled the committee.

For years the old guard of CTU had given lip service to working on education issues with community groups. But such coalitions often fell flat, largely because of union leaders' halfhearted participation. "In the old days, CTU really had to be brought kicking and screaming," said Rico Gutstein of Teachers for Social Justice, a local activist group with an anti-racist perspective.

"You always hear how labor works with community to get what they want, and then they leave," said Brown. "That coalition began to fall apart because folks didn't feel a commitment from the union to stand with us on the issues that impact our lives."

To make matters worse, CTU leaders were busy fighting each other. Things came to a head in 2008, when the president sought to have the vice president dismissed for financial impropriety, particularly lavish spending on meals and gifts. The vice president accused the president of similar spending. When the previous reformers were voted out in 2004, the union had had a $5 million surplus; now it had to cope with a $2 million deficit. "While teachers suffered from massive job cuts," said Al Ramirez, a teacher at Ruiz Elementary, "their leadership was not asleep at the wheel—they were joyriding."

Kristine Mayle, later elected CTU's financial secretary, was a special education teacher at De La Cruz, a middle school in

Pilsen. When she learned in early 2008 that De La Cruz was slated to close, Mayle worried what would happen to her students, who benefited from the school's award-winning programs for special needs students.

She also worried about her own uncertain future. This was her first job in the district. As a young, untenured teacher, she would be on her own to find a new job if the school got shut down.

She was furious at the lackluster response of CTU's old guard leadership. It was hard to get them to send a representative out to the school to calm nervous teachers, she said, let alone oppose the closing. "We called the union and they basically just told us to get our resumes together," she said.

But someone else did show up at De La Cruz to talk about fighting back. "They dropped some flyers in our mailboxes and said they wanted to have a meeting," Mayle recalled, "then showed up after school one day and said, 'Who wants to talk to us?'"

It was Norine Gutekanst, a third-grade bilingual teacher at a nearby school, and a couple of members of the Pilsen Alliance. "When we saw that De La Cruz was on the list, it was just natural, since it was our community, that we went over to see how we could organize the community to try to stop it," Gutekanst said.

"It was the beginnings of CORE," said Mayle.

Organization started to gel when Potter and Ramirez pulled together a meeting of about 20 people, borrowing the United Electrical Workers hall. Ramirez, a longtime union delegate (steward), had worked with Potter to make a documentary about the school closing fights. In the process, "we started running into other people who were ready for something, ready to fight back," said Ramirez, who would become CORE's co-chair.

Jen Johnson, a young history teacher and delegate, remembers, "It wasn't laid out what was going to come from that meeting. They figured this was the next step, to get more people involved in a new way."

The group decided to keep meeting and before long had adopted a name. "We weren't talking about running for office at that point," Johnson said. "We were thinking maybe we can get more people involved, we can help file grievances, involve community partners, show a different way to fight school closings and draw on the knowledge of community people.

"My personal sense was that there were some really experienced leaders in the room. They were doing things people in my building weren't talking about."

Study Hall

You might expect no less from teachers: one of their early activities was to form a study group, with the goal of understanding the issues and the players, in order to fight more successfully.

"I went to a study group to figure out what was going on in school closings in Chicago," said CTU's future president Karen Lewis, then a chemistry teacher. "I can't tell you how many times I've heard the 'there's nothing we can do' mantra. These teachers were talking about actually forming resistance."

One of the group's first and most influential readings was Naomi Klein's 2007 book *The Shock Doctrine: The Rise of Disaster Capitalism*, which describes how the New Orleans elite seized upon the opportunity of Hurricane Katrina to fire all 7,500 of the city's teachers and hand over the majority of its schools to private charter operators. "I think the best thing that happened to the education system in New Orleans was Hurricane Katrina," Secretary of Education Arne Duncan would later confide.

Klein argued that the rich and powerful use crises—whether real or mostly hype—to frog-march the public towards goals they would otherwise never agree to. The connections weren't hard to see, as waves of "crisis budgeting" were used to push charterization in Chicago.

The teachers also studied their union contract and the Renaissance 2010 plan. They read a Ph.D. thesis on the history of CTU. They read a piece called "Rethinking Unions," from the activist magazine *Rethinking Schools*, which argued for teacher unions to go beyond self-interest and embrace social justice unionism. And they read the newly published pamphlet *Hell on Wheels: The Success & Failure of Reform in Transport Workers Local 100*, about a rank-and-file caucus that won leadership of New York City's bus and subway union.

School of Hard Knocks

Although some of the teacher activists had worked together for years, the group was "very open and welcomed new people,"

CORE

recalled Bill Lamme, a social studies teacher who came to early meetings. He saw himself as a peripheral member at first, focusing his political energies on social justice activism with his students rather than the union. But he was impressed to find such smart, experienced people interested in getting something done together, not self-promotion.

The teachers "developed a collective body of knowledge," Lamme said. "They developed a group with a focused and common view of what had happened. They built themselves; they didn't just bring together disparate individuals."

It wasn't all readings. Among them, teachers in the group had years of knowledge and experience, which they systematically shared. Many were union delegates, veterans of fights within the union and with management, who had developed organizing skills and a solid understanding of what they were up against.

Some had been involved in PACT, a reform caucus that had held the CTU top officers' jobs from 2001 to 2004. So the group studied that experience and asked leaders from PACT to speak at a meeting. One of the key lessons: sentiment against the incumbents might be enough to sweep you into office, but it was not enough to transform the union once you got in. Veterans of that fight were wary of rushing into another electoral campaign. Instead, they stressed the importance of building a strong and independent caucus with active members in as many schools as possible.

Some in the study group were long-time socialists who knew the history of rank-and-file movements in other unions. And Potter's stepfather, Pete Camarata, was a founder of Teamsters for a Democratic Union. Members of the study group talked with local TDU activists and met with teachers union reformers, too—the Progressive Educators for Action Caucus, part of a coalition that

Starting from Scratch

Jim Cavallero had been a delegate for four or five years—a pretty disappointing experience.

"I was going to House of Delegates meetings and trying to bring information back to people, but there wasn't much to bring back, to be honest," he said. (The House of Delegates is the monthly meeting of representatives from each school.) "People in my school were starting to see the union as a waste."

And action? Forget about it. "I'd never been to a CTU rally," Cavallero said. "I'd never even heard of a CTU rally."

But he wasn't willing to give up. When he saw an article about a new caucus forming in the union, he recognized the author: Jesse Sharkey, someone he knew from the House of Delegates. "I tended to agree with the things he said," Cavallero said—so he went to the first meeting, liked what he heard, and got involved in CORE.

On the day-to-day level at his school, what did that mean? "Instead of me coming to people saying, 'This is what the union can and can't do for you,' I started saying it more as, 'What can we do? What can you do to be more involved—can you do this, can you attend this?'" Cavallero recalled. "Not just looking at the union as Merchandise Mart [the downtown commercial complex where the union had its headquarters], but asking what we as union members could do ourselves.

"And people did buy into it. It was a slow process, but they did. I had a lot of one-on-one conversations, and a lot of small group conversations with two to three people, trying to get them to come to a CORE event, or something one of our allies was throwing.

"When I started to see a change is when CORE ran for union leadership, and people started hearing the things Karen and Jesse were saying. They realized that was the kind of union they wanted: one where membership was involved. Not just trying to fight for a salary. Trying to fight for public education; trying to defend teaching as a profession." ☼

took leadership of the Los Angeles teachers local in 2005, and the Federación de Maestros de Puerto Rico. The Puerto Rican reformers had won leadership of their union, broken from the American Federation of Teachers in opposition to concessions, and in 2008 led a militant strike in defiance of a ban on public sector strikes.

CORE Goes Public

The teachers started spreading the word about CORE online with a June 2008 announcement. "CORE is a group of dedicated teachers, paraprofessionals and other champions of public education. We hope to transform our Union into an organization that actually fights for its members," they declared. "All of our jobs are on the chopping block with 400 teachers fired this year alone... What is our union leadership doing? CORE is fighting to stop these attacks on teachers."

The announcement laid out "a proposal for change that we hope you will help us develop and fine-tune," listing a four-point agenda: wages, improved benefits, better working conditions, and job security. Those sound like traditional bread-and-butter union issues—but under "working conditions" the new caucus included class size, high-stakes testing, an elected school board, and working with parents and students. Under "job security," ending school closings topped the list, and CORE proposed taking job actions and building a strike fund to stop the spread of charter schools.

The group planned a "Fight for Public Education" public event with Jinny Sims, past president of the British Columbia Teachers' Federation. B.C. teachers had struck illegally for two weeks in 2005, attracting the kind of community support CORE saw as vital—and winning smaller class sizes as well as a raise.

Gutekanst was impressed with the listening tours BCTF had sponsored to hear from parents and community members. The union "really connected with what were people's concerns, and what were their desires and hopes for education in the province," she said. About 25 people came out for a daytime meeting, and 75 in the evening. "We weren't talking about striking so much," Caref said, but about how Sims's group had "influenced the union to move in a more fighting, social justice direction."

CORE wasn't running for office yet, but it wasn't shy about

criticizing the incumbent administration. The caucus helped organize a protest at CTU headquarters, demanding the union "stop
the crooks and open the books," and calling for greater transparency and accountability to members.

Going to Every Meeting

The fledgling caucus decided to focus on fighting school closings. Although CORE was small and made up of volunteers with
full-time jobs, the group committed to attend all school board
meetings and closure hearings to speak out.

"Once we started going to board meetings, it totally changed
the character of who came out," said Caref. "We went to every
school closing hearing, every charter school opening, every board
meeting, and we said 'No. Stop now,'" said Lewis. Each time they
announced themselves as CORE, more members joined, especially from schools under attack.

Mayle and others had fought the closure of De La Cruz in
2008—they had students write letters to the board of education
about what the school meant to them and present them at the
school's closing hearing. Ultimately they lost, but they did win
an extra year of phase-out, so students could finish middle school
there in 2009 instead of having to transfer.

So Mayle's role at the hearings she attended was to prep everyone else—parents, students, and school staff—to "give them a
sense of what was going to go down, what talking points worked
with the board." Even when this didn't produce new CORE recruits, Mayle said, "we were the force showing that there were still
people willing to fight."

Special education teacher Margo Murray first got involved
with CORE this way. She was fighting for the therapeutic day
school where she worked. "This was a school serving black trou-
bled youth, children with severe behavior problems, who needed
therapy," she explained. "The CORE people were there, and I was
like, 'Wow, I don't have to do this by myself.'" Teachers and parents were able to stop the school from closing that year.

'These People Are Solid'

The individual relationships many of the teachers had formed
through their activism allowed organizational relationships with

community groups to develop organically.

"Initially people may have been a little hesitant to work with CORE due to the perception that they were young and inexperienced, but the fact is they were serious. They made up for their lack of experience with a fervor that was youth," said KOCO's Brown. People in the community organizing world would call him up, asking whether they should go to CORE meetings. "I'd say, 'Yes, these people are solid.'"

"The old CTU leadership never thought about the parents, ever. It was just bread and butter, take care of the members," Mayle said. "We realized our natural allies were the parents. It's super obvious. I don't know why anyone else didn't realize it."

A new coalition, the Grassroots Education Movement (GEM), began to come together. In addition to CORE it consisted of KOCO; Teachers for Social Justice; the Pilsen Alliance; Blocks Together, a community organization based in the Latino neighborhood of West Humbolt Park; Parents United for Responsible Education (PURE), a city-wide parent group; Designs for Change; and others. The coalition also included "a hodgepodge of occasional Local School Council presidents and members, depending on fights that were going on," said Potter.

"I remember a very long retreat trying to work out a mission statement for GEM that took all day," said Mayle. "The whole thing worked on consensus, true consensus." The group committed to democratic principles in education, the rights of every child, and the idea that schooling should "prepare students to deeply understand the roots of inequality and be prepared to act to change the world."

GEM became an important vehicle for mobilizing against the cuts and closures, organizing large protests that brought thousands to the streets in opposition to the school board's plans. Later the groups in GEM became the nucleus for CTU's Community Board (see Chapter 6).

Summit in a Blizzard

In January 2009, just months after the caucus formed, CORE sponsored a citywide "Education Summit" with the help of the groups in GEM. The summit served as a kick-off event for two months of intense organizing against impending closures.

Despite a driving snowstorm, more than 500 people showed up, representing 81 schools—far more than the 100-200 people organizers had anticipated. The crowd talked about closings, firings of veteran teachers, special education, student discipline, and how teachers and community members should work together.

The city had announced plans to close 22 schools in the next year but not said which ones. Right before the summit, the coalition's tireless meeting-going paid off. At one of the meetings, a parent organizer from Parents United for Responsible Education got hold of the closure list—"so we were able to announce the schools closing at this meeting," Mayle said. "We were the source of information for everybody."

Organizers had tried to ensure that each panel included a student, parent, or community member—not just teachers. Former charter school teachers and students exposed the myths about what was happening in charters. The momentum was so great that even CTU's administration felt compelled to participate, so CORE gave President Marilyn Stewart a speaking slot on one of the panels.

That forum was the moment the CORE activists realized their power, according to Johnson. "If 500 people can show up in the middle of a blizzard, then I think we are tapping into something that is real," she said.

Riding the momentum of the forum, GEM crystallized, and with its partners in CORE "began to mount some pretty intense fights against school closures" in early 2009, Brown recalled. The pressure was making the union's top brass pay more attention to the closures. "We invited the CTU leadership to join GEM," Lewis said, "and they came to a few meetings to learn how to organize."

In between citywide events, CORE activists were making connections with teachers, students, and parents school by school, helping them get organized to fight locally. "They brought their experience of how you do a campaign," Lamme said. "How to organize a demonstration, write a press release, confront the board at a board meeting—strategies for building your movement within a school." CORE didn't just build up a few charismatic individuals; instead, the caucus grew by helping more people develop leadership and organizing skills. "They stood behind people, not in front of them," Lamme said.

In late January, hundreds marched on a board of education meeting—opposing the 22 closures and demanding a moratorium on all closings and "turnarounds" (where the entire staff of a school is fired). The following month, CORE and community groups camped outside the district's downtown offices, keeping vigil in tents through the freezing February night. And the next day, hundreds packed a board of education meeting while hundreds more rallied outside. The coalition won a major victory, forcing the board to keep six of the 22 schools open.

But after the six schools were saved, the union leadership stopped working with GEM. "After the photo-ops ended, so did the union's active participation," reported Kenzo Shibata, an English teacher who later took charge of new media for CTU.

At CORE's convention in April, members held workshops and agreed on the group's principles. The caucus members chose five: a member-driven union, transparency and accountability, education for all, defense of publicly funded education, and a strong contract.

Discrimination Complaint

CORE continued to study the role of race in Chicago schools. As Caref remembers it, during a conversation about how the closures overwhelmingly hit African American students in high-poverty areas, someone pointed out that the district might also be targeting those schools to get rid of black teachers. "I said, 'Let me look that up, because I'm a research person,'" Caref said. She checked out the state statistics and sure enough: "When you compared the number of African American teachers at turnaround schools, before and after turnaround, there was a huge drop."

So in June 2009 CORE filed an Equal Employment Opportunity Commission complaint, on the grounds that turnarounds had a disproportionate impact on black teachers. Since 2002, the percentage of African American teachers in CPS had dropped from 39.4 to 31.6—a loss of 2,000 black teachers. "Essentially, a 'turnaround' constitutes a layoff policy that almost exclusively impacts African American teachers," CORE charged.

Wanda Evans, who taught at Orr High School for 11 years and had been nominated for teaching awards before it was turned around, said she felt "swept right out of the door." She suggested the turnaround plan was designed to save money by replacing senior teachers with lower-salaried new ones. "I'm completely offended by the way veteran teachers have been treated," Evans said. "It's like a fast food special: let's get a 2 for 1."

Socialize to Organize

"I went to my first CORE meeting before I ever went to a union meeting," high school teacher Adam Heenan said. He was invited by Xian Barrett, whom he met at a service-learning program in summer 2009—wearing a CORE T-shirt.

CORE held its meetings at Manny's Deli in those days. "We ordered food and talked about issues," Heenan said. "I was surprised by the way everyone let each other talk and gave their opinions. I hadn't really seen this before." Though busily organizing, the caucus was also still doing movie screenings and reading circles.

"I was impressed," Heenan said. "I said, 'I want to do this. I want to be a part of this. I want to get good at this.'" He took the lessons back to his school building, where he became an associate delegate and later head delegate.

Key to the delegate's job, in his view, is getting members involved in solving problems at their worksite—and getting them to socialize with each other, too. "My thing has always been 'socialize to organize to mobilize,'" Heenan said. "You can't expect people to march in the streets together if they don't even know each other's names." ⚙

CORE didn't end up winning the complaint, but the action was a foot in the door to start talking about the connection between school closings and racism—and to get veteran black teachers involved in the caucus. Under its old leaders, CTU had developed "a bad name in some of the black communities," Gutstein said. "What CORE has done is to concretely take up the struggle of the black community in particular."

When Arne Duncan came to speak in Chicago that month, CORE held a protest. "We had the statistics about the number of black teachers losing their jobs due to school closings," remembered Johnson. "We carried signs that were black outlines, the head and shoulders in black, to represent them."

After CORE activists reported via Twitter that they had been threatened with arrest for trying to enter, a flood of teachers responded with solidarity messages, offers to send bail money—and requests for directions to the picket line.

Issue by Issue

The caucus took up fights on other issues in the schools, too, such as the "20-day rule" that allowed schools to open or close positions 20 days into the school year. This was a way for the district to save money by adjusting to actual enrollment levels. But the savings came at the expense of a rocky start to the school year for students who would endure weeks of substitutes or overcrowded classes, or cope with program changes when their teacher was laid off.

"Does it really save money," Caref asked the board of education, "or does it just shift expenses to summer school or after-school programs which might not have been necessary if the school [year] had gotten off to a good start?"

CORE launched a campaign in the House of Delegates, successfully petitioning the union to hold a special meeting to debate the 20-day rule. The ruling caucus managed to block a vote, but CORE intensified its own public campaign on the issue.

The caucus also came to the aid of staff battling a bully principal. Prescott Elementary Principal Erin Roche was handing out record numbers of disciplines and terminations for weird reasons, in an effort to get rid of veteran teachers. One teacher was told she was fired for closing the blinds, among other "instructional weaknesses," *Substance News* reported; Roche was apparently convinced that "'research shows' children learn better in the sun." Teachers said Roche wanted to start charging tuition for Prescott's free pre-school program, to drive out the low-income Latino students; the neighborhood was in the midst of gentrification.

CTU members at Prescott reported that their union reps weren't helping them fight the harassment, instead advising that they find another job. So CORE and another opposition caucus teamed up to organize an afternoon picket, drawing 50 teachers, parents, and students, on the day of a Local School Council meeting in June. Days after the picket, district officials finally held a meeting to hear from teachers at Prescott and two other schools with problem principals.

CORE also began reaching out to reformers elsewhere, establishing the beginnings of a network. In summer 2009, a delegation traveled to Los Angeles to meet with reformers from L.A., New York, San Francisco, and Washington, D.C. (For more on the network that would grow from these beginnings, see Chapter 11.)

Time to Run

By the time the 2009-2010 school year rolled around, the writing was on the wall. With little more than a year under its belt, the caucus was already doing much of the work union leaders should be doing—but without its resources. "CORE decided if we were going to make a real change, we needed to take back control of the union," said high school teacher Adam Heenan.

Originally, "we just wanted to change the way things were done," Lewis said. "We thought we were making some progress because the president of the union came to some forums we held. We thought, 'Oh, this is great, we're going to see some fundamental change.'

"When that didn't happen, we decided we should run."

Lessons

⇨ CORE began doing the work of the union long before being elected.

⇨ Like-minded teacher activists found each other through action—fighting school closures—not just at union meetings. CORE sent an activist to every single school closure hearing.

⇨ The caucus developed alliances by working together with community groups as equals, not just asking for assistance with its own predetermined goals.

⇨ CORE activists were united by more than just their opposition to the incumbents. Through reading, conversations, and actions they developed a shared point of view.

⇨ CORE attracted new recruits by tackling issues teachers cared about. Filing a discrimination complaint, for instance, helped the caucus reach out to African American teachers who'd had reason to mistrust the union in the past.

⇨ CORE made activism enjoyable and welcoming to new recruits by making social events part of what members did.

⇨ Teachers with no prior experience learned how to organize by joining CORE's discussions and actions. As they shared their skills with other new recruits, CORE grew and could take on even more activities.

4

The Caucus Runs for Office

The United Progressive Caucus (UPC) had led CTU for 37 of the 40 previous years—at times even militantly, but those days were long past. Leaders seemed to have accepted that the tide of privatization was unstoppable and the best the union could do was manage its members' layoffs. They had made peace, of a sort, with the notion that management would get its way.

What's more, they saw the union's role simply as defending members on bread-and-butter issues—not as fighting for a brighter vision of public schools. When they couldn't do the former, they sat on their hands. "You would never hear from the union," said elementary teacher Nate Rasmussen.

CORE's win in the third-largest teacher union in the country happened very quickly, just two years after the caucus was founded.

Their victory was one-third inspiring vision—which is what drew Rasmussen to the fledgling caucus that was making a stand against privatization and over-testing. "CORE could verbalize that it was part of a different movement, and not just about our contract and whether we got a 4 percent raise," he said. "It was about quality teaching conditions in our schools."

The victory was one-third activist pluck, the willingness to jump into the trenches and start struggling on the issues. CORE activists didn't take a break from fighting school closures while they ran for office—in fact, they stepped up the fight.

And it was one-third good old-fashioned organizing know-how—the persistent list-making, numbers tracking, one-on-one conversations, and shoe leather, for which there is no substitute. "The genius of CORE, more than anything else, is that the people are organizers and they do it well. They think of details," said high school teacher Bill Lamme. "That's why even being such a new group, we were able to win the election."

Starting with Delegates

The caucus first started winning elections at the lowest rung: delegate. CTU's governing body is the House of Delegates, with about 800 elected members—one from each school and more from large schools. The House meets monthly, but its meetings had devolved to doing a whole lot of nothing.

Some CORE members had already been delegates for years; others ran and won. But once CORE had enough seats (around 20) to propose actions from the floor, union leaders responded by blocking new business from delegates. At times, the president would speak for as long as 40 minutes—counting on enough delegates to leave so there would be no quorum.

The next electoral step was a campaign for two vacant seats on the pension fund board of trustees. Every teacher seat on the board was held by a member of UPC, the incumbent caucus. CORE announced its candidates in July 2009, for an October election.

Jay Rehak and Lois Ashford were both veteran teachers, one white, the other black. Rehak had worked for the union during the PACT reform caucus's term in office. More recently he'd been watchdogging the district's fiscal choices, speaking critically in hearings about its sketchy investments in derivatives.

Ashford had taught for 16 years at Copernicus Elementary and joined CORE after she and the school's entire staff were laid off in a "turnaround" and forced to reapply for their jobs. She'd begun researching the pension board's actions at that point, realizing that the "pension was the only thing they could not take away." Now at another school, she was a member of CORE's steering committee.

Running for Pension Trustees

The CORE candidates went from school to school campaigning, bringing leaflets with pension information and talking to union members about what was at stake. "It was more of an educational campaign than a political one," observed CORE communications secretary Kenzo Shibata (later CTU's new media coordinator).

There was plenty to talk about. District CEO Ron Huberman was trying to bust teachers' pension down to a defined-contribution 401(k)-type plan—just as he'd done to Chicago transit workers in a previous job. Rehak and Ashford promised a more aggressive defense than that of the incumbent trustees, who were caving to both district and legislative attacks on teachers' pensions, they said.

But Ashford and Rehak weren't campaigning alone—the whole caucus got involved. David Hernandez, for example, was one of 10 from Social Justice High who stepped up to leaflet around the city. CORE made a spreadsheet of all the schools and broke out assignments by region.

At the October House of Delegates meeting, UPC moved to endorse the incumbent candidates for the pension board. This mattered because a union-funded mailer would go out with all the endorsed candidates' names on it. In the past these endorsements had been rubber-stamped. But CORE had a plan, an amendment to endorse all six candidates. All the opposition caucuses united behind it, and in a close vote, the motion passed: a good sign.

A Springboard

A week before the election, on a professional development day (when teachers are at school but students are not), CORE members canvassed hundreds of schools one more time. Two days before the election, the CORE candidates spoke once more at a board of education hearing, charging that CPS was trying to short the pension fund $100 million in a "last-minute, back-door" deal in the legislature.

It all paid off. In the October 30 election Ashford and Rehak were, narrowly, the top two vote-getters.

The pension campaign was important not only for its own sake—to salvage members' retirement—but also as a test of the caucus's reach and appeal. As the first union-wide election the caucus had contested, "it was a temperature check of how CORE was organizing," Hernandez said. It was also a springboard, building momentum for the higher-stakes campaign that would follow a few months later.

Of course, it was a signal to the incumbents, too. After the pension board upset, UPC collaborated with Huberman to publish new rules intended to curtail opposition candidates' ability to distribute literature or hold meetings at schools. The administration also challenged the eligibility of one of CORE's likely nominees for top office.

Forming the Slate

In a January 2010 meeting, 100 CORE members voted among five possible combinations and chose their slate of candidates for the union's top offices: Karen Lewis for president, Jackson Potter for vice president, Michael Brunson for recording secretary, and Kristine Mayle for financial secretary. The election would be held in May.

"First of all we wanted to have folks who were seen as really fighters," elementary teacher Norine Gutekanst said, "and we wanted to be representative of the different demographics in the union." The slate should also represent elementary as well as high schools and both veteran teachers and younger ones. It was a plus that Mayle had a background in special education, and that the four lived in different areas of the city.

The caucus also ran candidates for the rest of the executive board (dozens of seats) and for state and national union convention delegates. The next step would be a February-March push for 1,400 petition signatures to make the nominations official.

Potter, who was in a legal battle over his eligibility, withdrew from the ticket at the end of January, before the petition period was to open. He had taken a study leave three years before, and though he had kept paying dues the whole time, the incumbents now claimed he had not maintained the required three years' con-

CORE ran a slate of top officers in 2010: Jesse Sharkey, Michael Brunson, Karen Lewis, and Kristine Mayle, along with dozens for executive board.

tinuous membership. CORE activists believed he was in the right, but it would have been too risky to wait for the outcome of the court battle. Senn High School social studies teacher Jesse Sharkey stepped up to run for vice president.

Math teacher Carol Caref was in charge of the petition effort. "It wasn't hard to get signatures," she said, "but you actually have to go out and do it."

(The next time CORE ran, in 2013, the caucus tracked who signed the petition and used it as a recruiting tool. "If in some schools everybody signed it," said elementary teacher Sarah Chambers, "that's a good sign. If half signed it, that's a bad sign, and we would try to have a speaker go there.")

Making the List

It's one of the universals of organizing—the first thing you do is make a list. Alix Gonzalez Guevara, a teacher at Telpochcalli School, remembers staying up late transferring data about each school from a district-published book into an Excel spreadsheet: region, address, how many teachers, how many students. This became a Google document, an online spreadsheet available to everyone working on the campaign—all shared the same login information. "I would highly recommend the Google doc," Chambers said.

The schools were grouped by regions. Within each region, a couple of lead activists stepped up—people who lived or taught in the area—and took responsibility to find people to do outreach at each school. Then, whenever someone went out to leaflet or hold a meeting at a school, they'd document it in the central spreadsheet, so it was easy to track which schools had been visited a lot already and which needed more attention.

After each visit, activists also documented their current estimate of how support was running at the school. CORE didn't try to track where 27,000 CTU members stood individually; tracking was by school, an educated guess at the school's percentage of support based on conversations with members there, what the delegate said (and whether she was supportive), and how many had signed the petition to get CORE's candidates on the ballot. Relationships with delegates were a high priority. "We really tried to recruit the delegates," Chambers said.

On a typical visit, the CORE activist might spend a half-hour in the parking lot, talking with teachers about the issues. Then she would go inside, chat with the clerk if he wasn't too busy, stuff all the mailboxes with the latest CORE flyer, and leave a personal letter for the delegate, with a phone number to contact CORE if he wanted to set up a meeting. Where possible, she would try to arrange a group meeting so the officer candidates could meet teachers and answer questions.

"We had a group of 20 people who were available to go debate with the other caucus candidates at the schools," said Potter. "The decentralized approach allowed us to run circles around the opposition, who only deployed the four officers."

"We had an operation," Gutekanst recalled. "We really tried to blanket the city. We had a little mini-army of people who were willing to do that. And we were well-organized geographically around the city."

'A Mini-Army'

Chambers estimated 80 to 100 CORE members did these kinds of flyering visits, mostly in the morning or afternoon, before or after school. About 20 took some "personal business" days off to campaign. A few were out practically every morning or afternoon. The most work, of course, was done by the dozens of people on the slate, and the top officer candidates most of all.

CORE leafletted at Puerto Rican Day Parade.

Special education teacher Margo Murray, who made many such visits, reported it was the personal contact that won people over to CORE. "You have to spend that time talking," she said. "Reading it, sometimes they don't get it, but somebody they like or respect their opinion, making that personal contact—if they respect you, they're going to take a second look."

Over the course of the campaign, the caucus hit every school—most schools three times and some five times. The tracking made it easier to prioritize larger schools, ones that hadn't been visited much, those where CORE's forces were weaker, or, in some cases, schools where the caucus wanted to build up a base of potential activists. Lower priority was given to very small schools or to schools that were totally dominated by strong delegates from other caucuses.

At Caref's high school, the 10 CORE people met and split up the list of CTU members, with each person having 10 people to talk to. "People get interested in an election," Caref said. "There were people who hadn't previously been involved in CORE who took CORE lit to other schools and called their friends and were really campaigning for us. And that happened across the city."

"You always have to be putting it out there: 'these are the different ways you can participate,'" Gonzalez Guevara said. Someone might not be willing to hand out flyers, but "they would make some phone calls or host a fundraiser. You have to see what people are interested to contribute."

At CORE's general meetings—which grew more frequent, from monthly to every two weeks to once a week by the end of the

24-Hour Bins

One simple tool CORE came up with was the 24-hour bin. A member would volunteer to host a plastic bin outside their house in a place where people could get to it at all hours—on the front porch, for instance, or under the stairs. The bin would be stocked with the latest flyers, posters, or whatever literature CORE was distributing.

During the 2010 campaign there were five of these bins scattered around the city, making it easy for any volunteer to pick up the latest literature at any time. The system proved so handy that CORE kept using it for caucus flyers after the campaign was over. ☼

campaign—activists would report on the schools they had visited and pick up five or more new ones. Sometimes in these meetings they would role-play what to say when flyering—reporting what new questions they were hearing and brainstorming how to respond. (By the 2013 campaign, "we role-played in almost every meeting," Chambers said. These would be big meetings of 80 to 100 people, and the role-playing made them all "very, very knowledgeable about what was going on.")

CORE also held a half-dozen phonebanks, mostly targeting delegates the activists hadn't met yet. These cold calls proved helpful, Mayle said: "For those that weren't overly political, it helped get CORE's name out there." She and other callers got hold of delegates this way who hadn't even heard of the caucus yet—and by the time the election rolled around, some of these schools would end up voting CORE's way.

(The next time around in 2013, getting CORE's name out there was a non-issue, so the caucus didn't do many calls of this type; instead, mini-phonebanks targeted CORE's own members to make sure they came out to meetings. The ideal model was that used by Sue Garza, who by then led the Far South Side—one of the strongest regions. Each teacher took responsibility for five schools for the whole duration of the campaign. The teacher would stay in constant contact with the delegates those few months, and always know how each school was doing. Chambers

also recruited retirees: "They can go all day flyering. Or even family members! My dad flyered. Whoever you can get.")

Campaign Communications

Any time CORE activists visited schools or held campaign events, they gathered contact information: emails and phone numbers. Shibata contributed the email list he had built from his education policy blog, *thechalkboard.org*; others added members they knew would be interested.

Shibata estimates that at the height of the campaign the email list reached 5,000 and was one of the main ways CORE got its message out—letting members know every time the group organized a forum or rally. The caucus also had a busy blog displaying its many activities—in stark contrast to the union's official website, which didn't look like it had much going on. At the peak of the campaign the CORE site got 1,000-1,200 hits a day.

CORE also began publishing a newsletter not long after the caucus formed, printing each new issue in time to distribute at the monthly delegates meeting. At first the print run was small, but as the caucus grew more visible, starting to successfully move things in the House of Delegates and organize more of its own events, "people were actually asking for them," Shibata said.

So CORE started printing more copies and handing out whole bundles, giving people enough to distribute to each CTU member in their building. "At that time the union newsletter was big and glossy, with lots of pictures of the officers," Shibata said. "It worked like campaign lit essentially, and was a bit of a joke with the rank and file. We just did a four-pager, with information on what was going on in the schools—and more people were reading our newsletter than were reading the official magazine."

During the same period, Shibata started using Twitter to report, in real time, what was being said in board of education meetings. Since the meetings took place on weekday mornings when teachers couldn't go, "when I'd tweet them all that info, they could watch it in real time." (Or catch up on their next break.) CORE also started live-tweeting House of Delegates meetings. Oddly enough, Shibata said, the use of Twitter and other new media helped get CORE some press attention. "You can't get mainstream news coverage as a caucus within a union," he said. "But the fact that we were using these technologies often became a story, and got our name out."

As the election neared, CORE bought targeted online ads to make sure the caucus's logo and the election date popped up constantly onscreen for anyone who listed CPS as their employer on Facebook or was searching for anything CPS-related. This was not only a helpful reminder for supporters and fence-sitters—it was also a fun way to psych out the incumbents, making CORE seem ubiquitous. And when CORE's name was mentioned in a *Chicago Tribune* story about its EEOC complaint just before the election, the algorithm caused its banner ad to appear right beside the online story. "We had a huge spike in our page views," Shibata said.

Social and Fundraising Events

CORE's meetings grew steadily bigger, and sometimes split into regional meetings (North, South, and Southwest) "so the meetings could be a little more intimate," as Caref put it.

The caucus also sponsored plenty of fundraising events throughout the year. Among the most memorable were a night at a comedy club and one at a blues club, but others were as simple as a night out at a local bar with a door charge and raffle. These events did double duty—not only raising funds, but also serving as social opportunities to strengthen ties among the activists and welcome new folks in.

Official CORE members paid dues: $35 a year for teachers, $20 for paraprofessionals, retirees, and supporters. But that would have been nowhere near enough to pay for the campaign. Slate members were expected to chip in some of their own money, and the fundraisers held at least monthly were crucial. The campaign cost perhaps $30,000, spent mostly on printing and mailing flyers.

The caucus also continued to organize educational events. In the fall, together with Labor Notes and two AFSCME locals, CORE sponsored a day-long teach-in and strategy session called "Public Sector Workers Unite: Facing the Budget Crisis." And as the campaign heated up, realizing they still had gaps in their organizing know-how, the teachers went to school. The University of Illinois Labor Education Program set up five three-and-a-half hour classes for CTU activists in February, March, and April, focusing on union leadership, and a couple of dozen CORE members attended.

Round Two against Closings

Meanwhile, knowing that another round of school closings was coming, CORE had taken the offensive, starting off the 2009-10 school year with a bang. In an October press conference at City Hall the caucus unveiled a survey on the impacts of the 20-day rule and highlighted the alarming rise in student violence. CORE argued that CPS's policies—the rule and the school closures—were intensifying violence by destabilizing students' lives and communities, and by displacing the veteran teachers (overwhelmingly black) who knew the neighborhoods and students well.

The GEM coalition—CORE and community groups—called for an end to the Renaissance 2010 school closures onslaught in another press conference a few weeks later at a board of education meeting. Speakers included a displaced teacher, several former students, a minister who was on a local school council, a juvenile justice center worker, and the former vice principal of a military school who'd been forced out for resisting the district's push to make it selective-enrollment (students would have to compete for admission).

CORE held a summit at Malcolm X College in January 2010 to organize against the next round of closings—and to announce its slate for the election. The forum was scheduled for the day after CPS was supposed to announce the 2010 hit list of schools. CPS delayed the announcement, but 400 people came out anyway. The list was published a couple of weeks later: 14 schools targeted for closure, turnaround, consolidation, or phase-out.

Busy, Busy, Busy

It was a busy time. CORE activists continued their push to attend every school board meeting and closure hearing. After they persuaded a couple of aldermen to propose a moratorium on school closures, they had city council meetings to attend, too. They picketed the mayor. They held strategy meetings with GEM and caucus meetings of their own, and organized marches and candlelight vigils against the school closures. They showed up to support actions led by allies, such as parent group PURE's outreach at a district "New Schools" expo to showcase charter schools, and a march in defense of the public sector with bus drivers, AFSCME, and Service Employees (SEIU). They participated in the "No Games" rallies against bringing the Olympics to Chicago. All this was on top of the nuts and bolts of campaigning for union office.

But after all, CORE's activist identity *was* its campaign platform. All the meetings and actions gave the candidates plenty of

Sarah Jane Rhee, loveandstrugglephotos.com

opportunities to make their case publicly, tell their personal stories, and prove that their words were backed up by action. The CORE blog was packed with the latest videos and written testimonies from board of education meetings, school closure hearings, and other events. "We always made sure we wore a CORE button, a CORE shirt," Chambers said. People would "look around when a school's closing, and they wouldn't see any UPC."

The school closure fights were the reason Caref was able to get so many of the teachers at her school to join CORE, attend its events, and eventually vote for the slate. "We were always afraid we'd be next on the list," she said. (Sure enough, a couple years later, they were.)

"CORE was camping out all night in front of schools threatened to be closed, joining parents and kids," said Lamme, "while the union was sitting on its hands and being a little too generous in their compensation packages for themselves."

The board of education voted unanimously February 24 to close eight schools—but spared the other six that had been announced, including Guggenheim and Prescott Elementaries, which had mounted the most vigorous opposition. Unlike in the previous year, three aldermen had showed up to testify against the closings alongside CORE activists, and even the incumbent CTU leaders held a small picket and press conference outside.

'Name the Names, Huberman!'

The next day, CPS CEO Huberman announced a $900 million projected deficit and called on the union to re-open the contract—citing teachers' pensions, raises, and class sizes as targets.

CORE activists didn't miss a beat, announcing that they didn't trust the district's accounting. In a well-researched paper released a week later, the caucus pointed out that CPS had claimed a deficit each January or February for the past eight years—yet somehow the district always showed a surplus in its August audited budget. (CORE's early study group had learned about this kind of "crisis budgeting" routine when members read *The Shock Doctrine*.) Meanwhile, tax-increment financing (TIFs) diverted $250 million a year from Chicago's schools to subsidies for corporations.

And couldn't the savings be found in other ways, CORE argued, such as by scaling back executive salaries and cutting controversial bureaucracies like the Office of School Turnaround? CORE called on the district to open its books, and filed Freedom of Information Act requests with the state (and later a lawsuit against the district) for information on TIF money and line-item details on CPS's budget.

"Exactly why should we believe CPS's deficit numbers?" Lewis asked, pointing out that Huberman's harsh cuts would mean balancing the budget on the backs of students and educators. "Thirty-five students in a classroom is inhumane and it nearly guarantees school and student failure."

CORE and GEM organized a series of protests demanding that the district "name the names" of its outside contractors and reveal the cost of standardized tests and how much Huberman was getting paid. They pressed Illinois's attorney general to fast-track the information request. Students held a 13-school, 900-student walkout April 8; a few weeks later, student leaders returned to district headquarters again to call on CPS officials to rescind the awful budget. Senior Javier Lara Mendez said students wanted an "equitable, transparent budget with no cuts to students or teachers."

Solving Problems, School by School

CORE activists knew that in many schools, CTU had little presence. The Professional Problems Committees (PPCs) that were supposed to deal with school-level issues had fallen into disuse in many schools, and many delegate slots were empty. CORE members spent time going to these underrepresented schools to meet people. They worked to identify local fights to organize and involve them—such as schools where administrators were aggressively going after teachers.

"In our buildings we all tried to make an effort to get people to solve problems in the place they worked," said Adam Heenan, who joined CORE in the summer of 2009 and later became his school's head delegate. "If you can't solve the problem that's right in front of people's faces, you don't have their trust and you can't have the opportunity to solve bigger problems. But if you can do that, you've gained an ally and are more able to educate them on broader issues that may or may not have to do with the issue that's right in their face."

Lamme had already built that kind of trust over time. His school, Kelly High, did have a well-run PPC—he ran it. When he and the other teachers on the committee would receive complaints or suggestions, "we'd investigate, talk to the people involved," he said. Often "we got issues resolved before going to the principal."

And even though it was a big school, with more than 200 staff, "I got to know everybody," Lamme said—a personal strength. So when the election came around, it made sense that people came to him to ask, "Mr. Lamme, who do I vote for?"

"We didn't limit our issues to school closings, though that was our main campaign," Caref said. "We got people in buildings to join CORE; we got CORE people to take on campaigns in their school."

Many classrooms were short on textbooks, for instance. So after Potter found out about a state program to help teachers find unused textbooks in storage at other schools, CORE spread the word, providing instructions and a spreadsheet on its website to help teachers track down the books they needed. "CORE is teachers advocating for students," enthused caucus member Joyce Sia, "from fixing the CTU right down to hooking up schools with free textbooks!"

CORE was already "doing what the union should have been doing," said Lamme. "So when the election came, they didn't say 'Elect me and I'll do this.' They said, 'This is what we've been doing and we'll keep doing it.'"

Team of Rivals

Three other slates were also challenging the incumbent United Progressive Caucus in the election. UPC, primarily composed of older teachers and paraprofessionals, many of whom were retired or near retirement, was weakened by a dispute within its ranks, and had taken the union from a big initial surplus to a mounting debt.

The strongest of the other challenger groups was PACT, the ProActive Chicago Teachers led by Deborah Lynch, who had won the presidency in 2001. However, Lynch negotiated a concessionary contract in 2003, and members voted it down. A second, slightly better agreement was ratified, but the concessions were hard to swallow. PACT lost narrowly to UPC in 2004.

CORE tried to ally with PACT early on, but it didn't work out. "We had some common ground," Caref recalled, "but Debbie [Lynch] didn't take us seriously." And although some of CORE's key members had been part of PACT before, the two caucuses had different orientations. CORE was more political (more conscious of race, for instance), more activist, and more focused on organizing—identifying natural leaders and bringing them in. PACT was outspoken in its criticism of UPC, but not big on action.

Residual anger about Lynch's 2003 contract would hurt PACT's chances this time around. Still, PACT sounded a second voice of reform alongside CORE's.

UPC fought dirty, trying to shut down opposition caucuses from campaigning. "Leadership put out stumbling blocks, including telling bosses not to let CORE come to buildings," Lewis remembered. UPC put out flyers saying, "Stop Mob Action, Stop Radical CORE!" and even accused CORE of running for office just to give union money to community groups.

After UPC and the district tried to disallow union campaigning in the schools, PACT filed a free-speech lawsuit, winning a temporary restraining order in March. CORE activists started carrying copies of the order with them when they went to visit schools, prepared to stand their ground if anyone challenged their right to be there.

'Play It Safe,' Incumbents Say

UPC's presidential candidate, incumbent Marilyn Stewart, ducked a public debate with Lewis and made her case online, decrying the reformers' promises she called "pie in the sky." (The five presidential candidates debated in front of the House of Delegates, but the incumbents forbade recording, so few members heard it.) A moratorium on school closings? Hiring more counselors while Huberman threatened layoffs? Reducing class size? Winning a new benefit, paid and pensionable family leave? Halting the privatization of schools? Not a platform to save public education, the incumbents argued, but a series of "unrealistic pledges" made by naïve competitors.

Stewart campaigned on her experience, claiming that Huberman was "rooting for the rookies" over her team. She argued she could best protect the union's five-year contract—then in year three—which had achieved raises and slowed rising health care premiums.

The week of the election, UPC filed a lawsuit that grabbed front-page headlines, arguing that CPS's proposed class-size increases would violate fire codes. But it was too little, too late: UPC had come to be associated with charter school expansion and a decade that saw 6,000 members pushed out.

Right to the end, Stewart's caucus put forward a "play it safe" message. "You don't make radical changes in times of trouble," she told the press.

First Vote

As the May 21 election neared, CORE and its community allies in GEM were simultaneously building towards a big "Save Our Schools" rally downtown, May 25, against Huberman's budget cuts.

They created enough momentum to box UPC into a corner—the event was going to be too big to ignore. So CORE was able to move a resolution through the House of Delegates to support it. The rally got the union's endorsement "because they knew they couldn't stop it at that point," Mayle said.

CORE went all out on publicity, printing up 30,000 copies of a full-color poster featuring a beautiful, simple infographic—a bar chart comparing Huberman's claimed shortfall (then $600 million) with the $1.025 billion CORE calculated could be saved by cutting high-stakes testing, charters, contract schools, turnarounds, and TIFs, and drawing on CPS's reserves. The poster also included the rally info and CORE's name.

"We did a total blitz, made sure every school had these stuffed in mailboxes," Shibata remembered. Activists were going before school and after school and taking days off to deliver them. The posters were a big hit: easy on the eyes, featuring real information, and with a message of solidarity. Teachers were hanging them up in their classrooms. UPC got mad and called off a joint press conference with CORE. All good signs.

The day of the election, CORE activists and volunteers stood outside the doors at schools, handing out postcards reminding people to vote.

When the votes were counted, UPC got 36 percent and CORE got 33, with the other three slates splitting the other 31

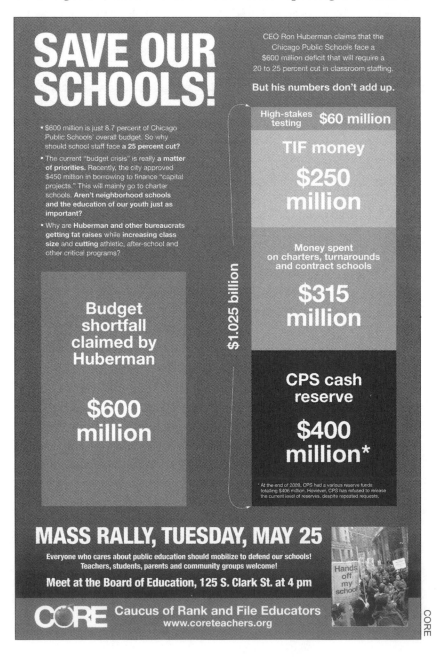

percent. About 71 percent of eligible members voted, a few points higher than turnout in the 2007 and 2004 elections.

'Save Our Schools' Rally

Close on the heels of the election came the hotly anticipated rally. "It was the first time the membership really showed up," not just a handful of activists but a large-scale turnout, Mayle said. "Everybody knew this was *the thing*."

Five thousand marched downtown, shutting down a main thoroughfare and getting Richard M. Daley's attention when the mayor's limousine got caught in the crowd. Bus drivers joined the march with signs saying "Huberman: Classrooms Are Not Buses"—a reference to the fact that they had endured cuts and layoffs when Huberman was the head of Chicago transit.

"We should have done this every year for the past six years," said Lewis.

"It was quite important, that rally, in helping us land in office," Gutekanst said later. "We were projecting an image of, 'This is what a fighting union leadership should do. We know how to fight and lead.'"

Run-off

Crucially, all the caucuses opposing UPC had agreed that if there was a run-off, all would throw their support to the non-UPC candidates. CORE had maintained respectful relationships with the other caucuses and did no public mudslinging against them. Some PACT leaders were thus quite helpful in the June 11 run-off.

But the insurgents couldn't assume it was in the bag. CORE activists repeated the outreach they'd done in the months before, visiting schools again to distribute literature and talk to people. This time they had new data to hone their targeting more precisely: the results from the first vote, showing turnout and the breakout of votes by caucus at each school. Gonzalez Guevara said she appreciated making the repeat visits—a chance to talk to more people and keep building the communication networks the caucus would need for its ongoing organizing after winning office.

CORE had started two years before with around 22 dues-paying members. By the time of the election, the group was around 400—still a modest organization among 27,000 teachers and paraprofessionals. But in the runoff, with 76 percent turnout, Lewis and the three other top officer candidates each won a decisive 59 percent, more than 12,000 votes.

"CORE has been doing the work of the leadership already," said Lewis before the win. "So we felt they might as well elect us."

The slate swept the other nine citywide offices and all the vice presidencies for high schools (six) and elementary schools (17). UPC retained a few paraprofessional slots on the executive board. CORE had well and truly won control of the union.

Caref, one of the newly elected area vice presidents, remembered, "And then we were all like, 'uh oh, now what do we do?'"

Lessons

⇨ CORE got practice and built momentum by running for lower level offices first.

⇨ Teachers were inspired to join CORE because of the group's bigger vision—not just bread-and-butter union issues but battling against racism and to improve education for all students.

⇨ CORE activists won fellow members' support by jumping into the trenches and doing the work of the union—even calling a big rally—not just talking about what leaders should do.

⇨ But winning office also required practical, old-fashioned organizing: making good lists, recruiting volunteers, going out to every school, holding thousands of one-on-one conversations, and carefully tracking support.

⇨ CORE held regional meetings after school, pizza/beer get-togethers, and social events as well as its union/political actions.

⇨ CORE set up a fundraising apparatus, selling tickets for events, T-shirts, and more. Many supporters dug deep into their pockets.

⇨ CORE made it possible to be involved on many different levels, from bringing a few co-workers to an event, to visiting another school with flyers, to running for office. A CTU member didn't have to choose the course of all-out activism that CORE leaders were exemplifying in order to contribute to the effort.

⇨ CORE made good use of Twitter and Facebook, but prioritized face-to-face connections at the schools.

⇨ CORE used an online spreadsheet (a Google document) available to all, so that information was not trapped in one person's head or on their computer.

⇨ CORE used role-playing to train members to respond to tough questions.

5

Getting Organized in Every Workplace

It was clear from the day CORE took the helm July 1, 2010 that to defend the students and the members—in fact, to save public education in Chicago—the union would need to be prepared to strike when its contract expired in 2012. The aggressiveness of the school board and the corporate education reformers pushed the union in that direction.

Leaders knew they would have to get parents, students, and community organizations on board to oppose the district's destructive strategy. They would also have to activate members for a contract fight like they hadn't seen in years.

But with the local's last strike more than two decades back, in 1987, most CTU members had never even participated in a vigorous contract campaign. No more than one in five had been around for the last strike.

So the new leaders had to transform their union culture: they had to inspire and train teachers in every school to step up. And they had two years to do it.

Organizing at the Building Level

A first step was to rebuild the union as a force within the schools, with delegates (the elected reps in each school) and rank and filers taking responsibility for enforcing the contract. This went hand in hand with educating all members about the huge threats facing the union and the students—but with the message that winning was possible if large numbers were in motion.

The new leaders realized that lack of confidence was their biggest barrier to organizing. Members knew that the sky was falling in on public education; they were not so convinced they could do anything about it. Many members believed that parents blamed them for bad schools.

So many, many union meetings at the schools were spent

trying to convince members that parents could and would support them. To build confidence and expand members' view of what was possible, they also needed *experiences* that proved parents would work alongside them and that victories were possible; Chapters 6 and 7 are about those fights. This chapter explains the internal organizing that was happening at the same time.

History teacher Jackson Potter, who became the CTU staff coordinator, sketched out their goal: "We'd like to see members taking on their principals and organizing with parents and the community before they so much as pick up the phone to call the union office."

One key decision was to start an Organizing Department, which had not existed before (as well as a Research Department). Elementary teacher Norine Gutekanst was tapped to head it. She hired four organizers from the ranks of teachers and paraprofessionals (one of them from the UPC caucus), who were able to go on loan from their jobs in the district. One experienced organizer from another union was also hired, Matthew Luskin from the Service Employees (SEIU) health care local in Chicago. Luskin, a former organizing director, was a strategist who had led large campaigns and managed teams of organizers.

Most of the new staff organizers had not received any formal training. Some went to their national union, the AFT, for basic organizing and communication skills. And after Luskin was hired, he gave classes.

"We trained ourselves," Gutekanst said, "how to move beyond just being an activist to actually convincing other people that through acting together we could accomplish something.

"We learned a very specific rap, a series of steps to go through in every organizing conversation, and tried to stick to it. It involves looking for issues that the member cares about and relating those to the situation the union is in.

"Then who is it who has the power that we need to take back? And how are we going to do that? By working together through our power in numbers."

Revitalizing Old Structures

Using their new Organizing Department, CTU leaders set out to breathe life into their old, existing structures and redefine

An Organizing Conversation

The *issues* part of the conversation means asking questions—and really listening to the answers—to learn what the member cares about, before asking her to take an action like coming to a meeting or signing a petition.

The fact that other members are fired up about, say, a threat to their pensions doesn't mean that's what motivates this person. Maybe she is most concerned about keeping music in the schools, or staffing for special education. Asking her to get involved will be more successful once the conversation is grounded in the issue she cares about most.

Agitation is where the member acknowledges that the problem she's just mentioned isn't okay with her, and isn't going to go away on its own. Telling her this is not nearly as useful as asking her the right question that gets her to say it herself; most of us generally remember what we said, not what the other person said.

Often a good strategy is to ask questions based on what the person has told you: "How long has that been going on? Is that okay with you? Do you see any way that's going to change if we don't take action?" Anyone who works a job knows the answers to these questions, but when we aren't organizing we often avoid facing them, just to get through the day. By reacting, the organizer can help the other person feel "permission" to be angry.

Someone's to Blame

Polarization is about pointing out that someone (an abusive principal, the board of education, billionaire "reformers") is responsible for creating these problems. Asking "Why do you think we're having this problem?" often gets to who is to blame. Often we feel our problems are just "the way things are." Realizing that bad conditions for workers didn't just fall from the sky can be very empowering: if someone made the decisions that made things this way, that also means they could *un*make those decisions.

Once the member is angry, the organizer had better be ready to offer some hope. The *vision of change* means talking about power in numbers and the union's plan to win, making the connection between the member's own issue and the action at hand.

It's important here to emphasize the idea of having a voice. People are motivated by many different concerns, but generally what unites them all is that the people making the decisions aren't the ones most affected by them. For workers, power in numbers is our only way to get a say.

The *commitment* part of a good organizing conversation is asking the member to decide to do something about it. Once she agrees with the vision of change and sees it as a way to win on the issues she's concerned about, asking her to take action is easy. She already believes that taking action with her co-workers is the only way to win; signing the petition, coming to the meeting, or voting yes to strike is the next step in that fight.

If someone is fearful or reluctant to act, it's a lot easier to help her through it when you're challenging her to act on what she believes—rather than being pushy about an action you are trying to "sell." Most people's reservations about taking action have real reasons behind them. Her fears aren't crazy, but still, things won't get better unless she gets involved. The organizer's job isn't to convince her that she's wrong about her fears, but that she needs to act despite her reservations. In other words, the organizer is helping her think like an organizer.

Of course, following this outline doesn't mean following a script mechanically—organizers still talk to people like human beings. But using the organizing "rap" as a guide ensures that the conversation actually moves the organizing forward, and the member isn't left feeling like her time's been wasted with a spiel or a gripe session.

A successful organizing conversation strengthens both the member and the union, and leads to action. ✿

---

the union's traditional roles. Those included the school-site representatives (delegates) and the monthly House of Delegates meetings, the Professional Problems Committees in each school, and a union position with the unfortunate title "district supervisor." Each layer had its problems.

At first, each organizer was responsible for 150 schools, grouped by region. (Later, when more organizers were hired, that number was cut to 100.) With about 250 delegate slots empty, out of 800, the organizers' first priority was to make sure that every school had a delegate. (Larger schools were supposed to have more than one.) Many schools had no delegate, or they were not doing the job, though the role of a delegate was minimal: to attend the monthly House of Delegates meetings and report back to fellow teachers.

The union had no accountability system to make sure that communication was happening—and boring House of Delegates meetings often produced little to report. Meetings were averaging only 400 delegates. (At the height of the strike, in contrast, 750 came, and the following year typically saw 650-700.)

Delegates had never been expected to write grievances. If a member needed one, the delegate would call a field rep from the Grievance Department. "People who took pride in themselves as good unionists and went to delegate meetings were fairly good at ensuring the basic bureaucratic functions of their role," said Potter. "Maybe 25 percent were doing it.

"But it goes back to the question around the role of delegates. Expectations were so low. Very few actually had the skills and wherewithal to organize their buildings to combat any sort of tyrannical decision-making by the administration, or deal with contract violations.

"What we wanted was a web of people to facilitate everybody being involved at the school level."

So once the CORE slate took office, the duties of a delegate changed. "It was organizing," said Financial Secretary Kristine Mayle. "And educating. We started education at meetings that was more substantive. We started talking school funding and the power structure in Chicago and charters and big picture reform stuff. That's what started the delegates being more active."

To recruit new delegates, organizers went to schools to talk to members in the parking lots or as they were signing out. They called after-school meetings to explain how leaders saw what the members were up against, and they cajoled people to take on the job. If more than one person stepped up in a school, an election was held.

At the same time, the Professional Problems Committees needed to be rebuilt; they had fallen into disrepair in three-quarters of the schools. These are school-based committees of three to five, mandated by the contract and led by the delegate, that are supposed to meet monthly with the principal to resolve issues before they become grievances. They are elected annually, with members serving as the eyes and ears of the delegate around the building.

"We talked to people very directly about what we saw as the changing role of delegates," Luskin said. "Delegates would have to be leaders in their building and organizers of their staff, parents, and school community."

Training about what it meant to be an organizer was specific.

A Turnaround of Teacher Opinion

In a school turnaround, everyone is fired and has to reapply for their jobs. This happened at Curtis Elementary, where Andrea Parker teaches. A private company called AUSL took over managing the school—and from now on, the principal said, everyone had to work until 3 p.m. instead of 2:45.

The school had no delegate, but union headquarters got word and sent someone out to hold an election. "The principal wanted to pick someone she liked to be delegate, but she was absent that day," Parker said. "I raised my hand because I had tenure. They elected me."

Just like that, Parker started going to delegate meetings. "Wow, I felt so empowered," she said. "I got so much knowledge about things I wasn't aware of." For instance, it turned out "we were not supposed to be working till 3 unless we had a meeting with staff and we voted on it. She did it illegally."

Of course, violations of law don't fix themselves—it would take action by the members, or at least the delegate. "The majority of the teachers were new and said, 'I don't care,'" Parker remembered. Some even got upset, accusing her of being mean to the principal.

Still, knowing that "when you waive one part of the contract, you waive it all," she braved the conflict and filed a grievance anyway. "I said, 'We have to show our union means something.'" It worked. "We got $2,000 back per teacher, on average—including those who were mad at me," Parker said. "Everybody took the check."

There was a big divide between teachers who had worked at the school before and those who were new since AUSL took over. One teacher was sure she could never be fired. Parker challenged her to come to just one union meeting. She did—and was impressed.

"That's why I had 80 percent of my staff come to that march downtown" in May 2012, Parker said. "They realized, 'I'm being propagandized against.'

"That first year we were a turnaround school, 10 teachers were fired for being 'not compatible with the AUSL way.' When people saw that—students' scores not getting raised, people getting fired—they realized Ms. Parker is not the bad guy after all." ✿

On a practical level, the union put all the files a delegate would need on a USB flash drive: the contract, the constitution, roles of delegates. More important was the organizing attitude.

"Many delegates would complain about members who

wouldn't attend union meetings in the school," Luskin said. "We encouraged people to think about *why* people weren't coming to meetings. Was it the schedule, for instance?

"Many delegates were mad that people weren't coming to 'get important information.' But 'getting information' can make for a pretty dull meeting. And how important is it really for me to be there, if it's just for you to pour info at me? We pushed people to instead make meetings into a place where issues were raised and plans were made."

The organizers came to know all their delegates: who had a lousy principal, who rarely ran union meetings, who had their building solid. Organizers attended school meetings to listen to members and get them to take action, not to "serve" them. The organizers were a resource for those who wanted to fight but needed support and training. The goal was to have a school meeting once a month before or after school, to discuss both building-level issues and larger ones.

"We decided there are other things you can do besides file a grievance," President Karen Lewis said. "We started talking to people about what you could do. We started doing very simple things—let's wear red on Friday to show our solidarity, to show we support one another. Even people you don't get along with, start talking to them. If you start communicating with one another, you build strength within your building."

"We spent a lot of time talking with people about the 'whys' of these activities," said Luskin. "We tried to avoid just shallow mobilizing—if we were asking delegates to do something we tried to communicate the thinking behind it. For example, we wear red shirts to show the people who are scared in your school how much support they would have, and to make sure the principals are talking about how widespread it is."

In other words, the union wanted to make the new strategy very visible. The idea was to win members over to the strategy, not just turn them out to a string of events.

"That big picture discussion of what we are up against and what it would take to win was a key part of school visits," Luskin said. "This was not the style of organizing where you start with the lowest-common-denominator issue and fight for that, hoping people will get bolder later.

"We said that *your* jerk of a principal was linked to the increased number of bad ratings teachers were getting systemwide, which then was linked to the overall corporate vision of education reform. We said yes, we need to organize to fight on whatever the issue is at your school, but there is no winning on your issue if that doesn't feed into a citywide fight to change the whole environment we are in."

To prod into action members unaccustomed to an active union, organizers would come to the schools with long lists of asks—sometimes too many, said Debby Pope, a retired history and ESL teacher who came to work in the local's Grievance Department. "Can you organize a busload of teachers and parents to the next demo, can you wear red on Fridays, can you get the PPC together and meet monthly with the principal, can you include the paraprofessionals in your meetings, can you talk to the parents at report card meetings?"

Giving members lots of options created many ways for people to get involved in the union—"to broaden people's sense of what counts as 'union issues' and what tactics were fair game," Luskin said. "We gave priority to activities that had members mobilizing their co-workers or doing direct outreach to parents. We thought good experiences at those would build people's confidence and skills, which would be key later."

Training the Delegates

Training of delegates was amped up and now happens every fall and spring. The first delegate training, in late fall 2010, drew 300 and introduced the notions of member-to-member communication and expanding the number of people who identify with the union and can help mobilize. It was a significant shift from delegate training that had primarily covered "know your rights" topics like contract training or board of education processes. Now the training was on how to organize others to enforce and expand those rights.

Labor educator Steven Ashby suggested that the union make a video to talk about CTU's history, introduce the new leaders, and connect the history to today's attacks. The Labor Education Program at the University of Illinois worked with the union to make the 11-minute video, which included photos of CTU mem-

CTU trains old and new delegates.

bers marching against banks in the 1930s. "It harked back to a militant past that our membership was not aware of, and it pointed to future fights and what it was going to take," said Gutekanst. The video was shown at trainings, distributed to every delegate, and shown in school meetings.

Delegates at the first training also watched a video made by the Teamsters when reformer Ron Carey was president in the 1990s, about how to do member-to-member outreach.

"We were not particularly successful in getting that point across at the first training," Potter remembered. "It was too abstract. But the idea stuck with us, and we were able to figure out the best combination of practical steps. We gave delegates rosters of members in their buildings. We taught them how to figure out who has relationships with particular departments, who should talk to the parents, how to develop the phone tree."

At one point the trainings were expanded beyond delegates—everyone from the Local School Councils was invited, and later, members of the Contract Action Committees (see Chapter 8). Since the strike, all PPC members have been invited, too. The idea is to build teams in each school, rather than depending on individual delegates. In 2013 some high school students were invited to the spring training.

The Saturday sessions had plenary panels of speakers from inside and outside the union, such as community partners, but the heart of the matter was the workshops. Some were on shop floor skills: how to file a grievance, how to have an organizing conversation, how to build a strong PPC, contract enforcement. Others trained members in the skills they would need to take on the anti-teacher agenda in the outside world, including coalition-building; fighting back against school closings; fighting charter proliferation; ways to win full funding of schools; getting engaged in city council and state legislative fights; engaging parents to save our schools; and research: learning and using it.

Sometimes workshops were set up geographically, with teachers from the same CPS "network" talking with their district supervisors about common issues such as closings or overcrowding. Members of community organizations like the Kenwood Oakland Community Organization (KOCO) and Blocks Together co-led some workshops.

Over time, the workshops were synchronized with the stages of CTU's various campaigns: "How to Move Co-Workers and Assess Strength in My School" (in the lead-up to the strike vote); "Campaign Planning and Messaging" (as the school closing fight heated up); "Organizing with Our Allies." Each workshop sent delegates home with planning materials, to help them think through ways to put the organizing strategies to work in their buildings.

In March 2011, leaders of UNITE HERE, the Service Employees, and the Operating Engineers, who also represented

New Delegates Step Up

English teacher Jerry Skinner became the head delegate at Kelvyn Park High School in late January 2010, just five months before CORE was elected. A new principal had just bullied the previous delegate out of office, and a CORE member at the school, Liz Brown, encouraged him and fellow teacher Eric Wagner to step up. Brown had already introduced Skinner to Jackson Potter and John Kugler, whom Skinner describes as a "roving all-city field rep and pit bull," and Skinner attended CORE's big January 2010 Education Summit.

"It was designed to educate people like me," Skinner said. "We heard from people already active in other schools. I went to the workshop on bully principals and taking back our schools."

Skinner and Wagner started calling frequent union meetings after school, both on and off campus, which grew from 10 out of 90-some teachers to 30 or 40. Up to 30 teachers at a time have come to Local School Council (LSC) meetings to confront the principal over such practices as rearranging teachers' schedules midway through the semester, cutting extracurricular programs, and terminating staff.

At one point, in April 2010, the two delegates had managed to wangle a meeting with a top CPS official for their "network" (CPS's former term for a geographical division of the city). They wanted him to hear firsthand from teachers about the problems at Kelvyn Park. The night before the meeting the official insisted on having the principal present. Wagner told him flatly no, knowing the purpose was intimidation.

Ninety percent of the tenured teachers turned out the next day to give the official an earful. "Eric and I couldn't have done it by ourselves," Skinner said. "We couldn't have countered his arguments. We needed the special education teachers there. We needed science teachers there. All the teachers would give their precise individual expertise. When the CPS official tried to argue that the school was adequately funded in one area of instruction, a literacy teacher would say, 'No, that's a different budget.' The expertise is in the whole union.

"It was a watershed moment early on."

Skinner says he believes new principals always try to run a school on a tight budget to impress their superiors. He discovered that the principal had returned $300,000 earmarked for Kelvyn Park to CPS.

To get the money back, he and Wagner decided to go over the principal's head to her bosses. Skinner went to an October 2010 board of education meeting with the parent president of the LSC, two girls' volleyball players, and two parents. After the girls testified about their season being canceled by the principal, Schools CEO Ron Huberman set up a meeting with the head of CPS Sports, and this led to a meeting between Wagner and the principal's immediate supervisor. "All of a sudden we had $300,000," Skinner said.

Turning around Transformation

In 2011 Kelvyn Park became a "transformation school," which means it gets extra money from the state. When the designation was announced, Skinner was skeptical. He called a union meeting and Kugler made sure five members from two "turnaround" schools—where the whole staff is fired and must reapply—were there.

It turned out that the same CPS department in charge of turnarounds (the Office of School Improvement) was also in charge of transformations. The visiting teachers told of the ugly experience of turnarounds: teachers not rehired were often blacklisted and did not get rehired at other CPS schools.

"This is just one instance of the culture of sharing information and looking out for each other that CORE has promoted among the membership," Skinner said. "In this case it helped us insist on more resources in the classroom—rather than more resources for administrators—and better safeguards for members' jobs when we became a transformation school."

He adds, "You have to have someone on your side in every possible forum—the Local School Council, the PPC, the Professional Personnel Leadership Committee (PPLC)—so that there's no pathway through which a principal can push a hostile agenda without meeting resistance.

"The LSC, PPLC, and PPC all have members elected by staff and a contractual-legal foundation, so the principal is obligated to meet with us as equals, where we have the power of investigation and can ask the tough questions." ⌂

workers in the schools, were brought to speak at the delegates training, along with the executive director of KOCO. (Custodians, janitors, security officers, lunchroom workers, special education classroom assistants, and engineers are among the CPS workers represented by other unions.)

"We put our labor allies on the same plane as our community allies," Potter said. "We did that on purpose to show our members that we had allies in our buildings and that we had to think about how to include them in our tactics."

The next year, community allies led CTU workshops for teacher representatives on the Local School Councils. (Read more about LSCs in Chapter 6.) Student, religious, and community leaders addressed the full sessions. "We were intentional about using every opportunity to make sure those folks were included," Potter said.

A New Job for District Supervisors

To help activate the 800 delegates and the PPCs, the union decided to revive and transform the long-existing district supervisor system. The DS was an appointed position with minimal duties and a stipend of $100 a month. Members of this "sleepy patronage army," as one member called the DS structure, were briefed after executive board meetings and were supposed to remind delegates in their areas to attend the House of Delegates. Debby Pope, a delegate for nearly 15 years, said, "I got exactly one phone call in that whole time."

The new leaders dismissed the less-engaged DSs and increased the total number to 37 (later 49). Each was responsible for nine to 23 schools, or for delegates from a citywide job category such as clerks or teacher assistants.

The new DSs were tasked with contacting delegates monthly, listening to the issues from their buildings, responding with assistance as needed, and engaging delegates in the union-wide actions going on that month. The DSs checked in with delegates about turnout from their buildings for events and other organizing asks, and they sent reports to the Organizing Department, with each DS reporting to a top officer or staffer.

In the past, the DSs' assignments had not necessarily been geographically logical. The new leaders took CPS's map, where schools were divided into areas or "networks," and split most networks into two parts. The two DSs for each network could work together and cover for each other.

Paraprofessional DS Charlotte Sanders says that after she confers with delegates and talks with members at school meetings, she passes information back to union staffers who can help tackle the problems. Depending on the issue, that might mean staffers from the Grievance Department, the Organizing Department, or both. "Say at a large high school, teachers are not getting their prep period," Sanders said. "You might need someone from the Grievance Department to go out, and someone from Organizing

A CTU delegate training.

Ronnie Reese, CTU

to say 'You don't have to take this.' It's a team effort to cover all the bases."

DSs were trained in how to have an organizing conversation. They began to meet monthly, a week before House meetings, with the financial secretary and Organizing Department leaders.

A typical agenda includes an overview of what is happening in the district, followed by a training or an activity to get them thinking and working like organizers. They might be asked, "Based on your conversations with your delegates, how likely do you think it is they will do x, y, or z? What tells you that?"

Then, in a Q and A session, DSs can tell leaders what they're hearing in the schools, report back on successes and challenges, and ask questions about bargaining or contract violations.

Strategy is a big part of the meetings. "We are transparent in our thinking about how to build and how to move people," Mayle said. If leaders were contemplating civil disobedience, for example, "we'd bounce these types of things around with the DSs to get buy-in, make adjustments to see what would work in the schools, and make sure that the DSs had a deep understanding about *why* we were using the tactics we were and what we were hoping to get from them."

When it came time to build for the strike, leaders started very early with the DSs, laying out their estimates on what it would take, and their goals. "Even when leadership was still being cautious about using the 'S' word," said Mayle, "the DSs read between the lines and knew we were building to a strike before we were able to say anything publicly."

The DSs became a crucial level of organization and an essential communication system. As contract expiration neared, they were to report up the chain how well the Contract Action Committees were doing (see Chapter 8), and how many members were wearing red on Fridays. During the strike they would act as coordinators, overseeing eight to 12 schools apiece, visiting each picket line daily, and then meeting as a body each day of the strike.

Summer Interns Learn to Be Leaders

For six weeks in 2011, the union hired seven members at $450 a week as summer interns, with the goal of training more leaders/ organizers. In 2012, to increase the proportion of people of color in leadership positions, of the 25 interns hired, 23 were black or Latino. Special attention was paid to recruiting paraprofessionals, since members in these jobs were often underrepresented. The group included both veteran activists and young members just beginning to think about the union.

Leaders knew they needed to recruit applicants via appeals to the general membership rather than just among activists they already knew. "It helped bring in people who were just becoming union activists, and people with a base where we were weak," Luskin said. "Lots of applications came in from people we never would have met otherwise—many of them very strong."

Using discussions and role plays, Luskin trained interns in the basics of organizing and power dynamics in the workplace, and they learned about school financing and the national anti-teacher agenda. They studied Martin Luther King, Jr.'s "Letter from a Birmingham Jail" and Cesar Chavez's "A Union in the Community." They learned how to have a doorstep conversation and how to get invited into a member's home. They learned how to listen to fears and reservations, and how to address those concerns and move people past them. They knocked on members' doors at home, looking for those who would be willing to organize a house meeting or work on a community forum, in their own neighborhood, on the union's vision of improving education.

Interns were teachers, paraprofessionals, and clinicians. In 2013 the program would be expanded to include high school students, community activists, and a charter school teacher whose school had recently unionized with CTU support. Organizers were on the lookout for those who had shown their chops as leaders during the strike. All members were invited to apply and some were specifically asked to.

Many of the earlier interns were hired as organizers or later became strike coordinators or DSs; some DSs became executive board candidates in 2013. "It's like a pipeline, a new layer of leadership," Mayle said.

It's worth contrasting the goals of the intern training to the way most unions hire members for temporary organizing roles. Usually such hiring is done when a campaign needs more doorknockers. Leadership development, if any, is a byproduct. CTU's program, in contrast, was primarily about developing new leaders.

Social studies teacher Tim Meegan, an intern in summer 2013, said he'd learned how to encourage people who agree with the union's goals but are reluctant to take action. Knocking on doors, he registered voters, identified community leaders such as block-club presidents, and promoted community meetings to make an action plan on school closings and budget cuts.

"The union is not saying 'here's what we're going to do,'" he explained. "We're calling a meeting to say 'what can we do about it?' The union can't fight this stuff by itself."

Interns gathered petition signatures in 2013 for a graduated income tax in Illinois (one of only a handful of states with a flat tax). CTU is part of a statewide coalition to change the constitution to allow this tax. "We know at the end of the day you can't fight austerity without changing the distribution of wealth," Potter said. "It's a practical campaign that allows you to talk about the root cause of the problems we're having."

Grievance Department

CTU grievances were traditionally handled by full-time staff in the Grievance Department, and still are, but delegates have been trained and encouraged to write grievances rather than always calling a field rep. The separation between organizing and contract enforcement still exists, though, and the union is "grappling with how to make it more seamless," in Potter's words.

He believes it was right to start by forming an Organizing Department and put the emphasis there. "Field staff had become very traditionally oriented," he said, "talking almost entirely about ways you can protect yourself from child abuse allegations or file grievances if you're retaliated against. But most members didn't face that. It was important for us to disrupt that and to send people out who could engage more broadly and figure out what was making people tick—and how to deal with *those* issues."

Of course, the issues at the top of members' minds weren't necessarily contract violations. They were everything from bullying principals to charter school expansion to the loss of black teachers to wanting more special education services. Members wanted things they didn't know they could look to the union for. Part of organizers' job was to change the perception of "union issues."

CORE Sticks Around

After the CORE slate was elected, a majority of its leaders were involved in running the local, as executive board members, staffers, DSs, or chairs of union committees. But there was never any doubt that CORE should remain an active caucus.

Before the reformers knew they would win, they had discussed how important it would be to keep CORE going. Those who'd been involved in the earlier PACT caucus (see Chapter 3) knew that leaders needed a mechanism for keeping in touch with rank-and-file sentiment. They were well aware of the inevitable conservatizing effect of holding office, with a big institution to run and with leaders no longer experiencing the day-to-day problems of classroom teachers.

"Even though the officers don't want to become disconnected, their reality is different from the reality of a teacher slogging it out on the ground," Pope said. "If you can always go to the bathroom when you want...

"It's also very good to have non-officers out there to be eyes and ears in the schools, what's playing well and what's not. And you need to have people who will be critical."

"CORE can raise red flags and alarms, have the pulse of the members," Potter added, "be a critical conscience to raise concerns when the union is making bad choices."

So the caucus, including the new top officers, continued to meet. In the early months meetings were less frequent and not so well attended. Missteps in dealing with the legislature in spring 2011 (see Chapter 7) were a wake-up call that convinced everyone CORE needed care and attention.

"There was a period in the first year when those of us on the CORE steering committee were now working at the union," Potter remembered. "The number of challenges and crises was overwhelming. Our ability to manage both organizations simultaneously was limited at best. There were missed opportunities.

"But we still maintained a regular set of meetings and basic communication; we had internal discussions around issues. Those things did not vanish; they were in place. That allowed our next layer of activists to step up into the vacuum and say, 'Hey, this isn't working as well as it needs to.' We came to the conclusion we needed to diversify the steering committee with more rank and file and less staffers, so work would get done and people would have more leadership opportunities."

The caucus continues to meet once a month, or twice a month when the situation demands, with an annual convention in the fall. Several hundred members pay dues (still $35 a year for teachers, $20 for paraprofessionals), with 30 to 40, and up to 75, attending a typical meeting. Any CTU member, active or retired, may join—and spikes in activity lead to more members wanting to get involved.

"Folks in CORE tend to be more political," said Gutekanst. "Some have been around a while. We see this is a long-term project. CORE has the possibility of providing more institutional memory, and somewhat of a check and balance on leadership." At the same time, CORE includes many of the youngest activists in the union—the mix of generations is one of its defining characteristics.

The continuing existence of CORE shows members that what changed at CTU wasn't just the feistiness of the leaders at the top. New activists can see the role of rank-and-file leaders in determining the union's direction. It's clear that the leaders at the top came out of a much bigger group, and in CORE, new activists meet peers who feel ownership of having moved the union onto its current course

So CORE continues to function as a recruitment and training ground for new activists, and, of course, as an election vehicle (elections to the pension board, as described in Chapter 3, are held every year).

CORE can also take actions that are more appropriate for a caucus than for the union. In the summer of 2011 CORE sponsored a national get-together for teachers who wanted to fight the corporate "education reform" agenda, inviting both local officers and members of opposition caucuses. In summer 2013 a larger conference was held (see Chapter 11).

✧

The delegate trainings, the summer intern program, and the building meetings described here were key to spreading skills and the organizing mindset among a larger subset of the members.

Members could choose from a wide array of ways to be involved.

"Before, people got the newspaper or the information the union sent in the mail, and they would read it and throw it to the side," Sanders said. "Now they are more vocal. It's not like, 'I just pay my dues.' It's more of an inclusion."

But the internal organizing was only a part of how CTU got members to step up. The union simultaneously had to strengthen its relationships with parents (Chapter 6) and carry out a daunting number of campaigns, often simultaneous, against attacks from the legislature, the mayor, and the school board (Chapter 7).

More than anything, it was these experiences—speaking to parents about the board's attacks; the rallies where teachers and parents were arrested together protesting against bankers; seeing a principal back off due to a petition or action at a staff meeting— that built the confidence that allowed members to see organizing as the way to go and a strike as a viable strategy.

Lessons

⇨ CTU's new leaders saw their first priority as developing rank-and-file leaders who could get their co-workers involved at the school level, so they created a new structure, the Organizing Department, and hired and trained a crew of organizers with that specific task. These they drew primarily from CTU's own ranks but supplemented with experienced organizers from elsewhere.

⇨ CTU was frank about the change in course, recruiting delegates to a new conception of their role rather than the old, minimal one. Not just the tasks but also the thinking behind each task were laid out clearly for all to see.

⇨ CTU trained a thick layer of new leaders to think like organizers. Trainings were expanded to bring in the largest number of potential leaders, in order to build teams in each school.

⇨ While many citywide campaigns were launched, local initiatives led by members in their schools were encouraged, supported, and highlighted to others.

⇨ CTU made use of its existing structures—ones members were familiar with—even though these had been dysfunctional in the immediate past: the monthly House of Delegates meetings, the district supervisors, the Professional Problems Committees. At the same time, leaders didn't try to fix everything at once; they left the Grievance Department to tackle later.

⇨ CTU developed an intermediate layer of leaders, the district supervisors, who played an essential support and communication role between officers/staff and delegates in the buildings.

⇨ CTU consciously trained a new layer of leaders through the summer intern program, and recruited members of under-represented groups to fill those slots.

⇨ Recognizing the inevitable pressures on officers, CORE members continued to function as a caucus that could help correct course when necessary—and provide a training ground for still more leaders.

6

Community Partners

One of the most remarkable things about CTU's 2012 strike is that these educators won community support in a national political climate that was not simply anti-union but anti-teacher. A poll conducted by We Ask America in the strike's final days found that a majority of Chicagoans—including 63 percent of African Americans, 65 percent of Latinos, and 66 percent of parents of school-age children—were supporting it.

Community support, however, went far beyond mere favorable opinions. Neighborhood organizations throughout the city played a critical role in both drumming up support for the strike and coordinating on-the-ground support. Action Now, the Kenwood Oakland Community Organization (KOCO), the Albany Park Neighborhood Council, and the Logan Square Neighborhood Association pulled members together to canvass their neighbors in the lead-up to the strike. They held town-hall forums, organized day camps for out-of-school children, turned out members en masse to downtown rallies, and organized pro-CTU press

Different Types of Alliances
(Excerpted from CTU training materials)

Weakest—"Please come support us!" Some people will come help, because they like us or because it is "the right thing to do."

Medium—"You help us on *this* and we'll help you on *that!*" Scratch each other's backs: It does help for your ally to know that you will return the favor. It's stronger than a one-way relationship, but people will only go so far just to help you with your issues.

Strongest—"We're in it together!" Solidarity: We are both being harmed. Working together and supporting each other is the only way to fix it. "Supporting you helps me win, too." ☼

conferences and rallies of their own (see details in Chapter 9).

Why did community groups feel so compelled to support the strike? It was simple, said Jitu Brown, a KOCO organizer: "Parents knew their schools were being sabotaged, and they knew that teachers were standing up against that, so they stood with them."

In addition, said Raul Botello of the Albany Park Neighborhood Council, which functions on the Northwest Side, it was important that CTU was willing to call out the school board's racism. "They were talking and speaking the language of parents and youth," he said. "The people felt their fight."

Parents didn't just see the strike as a way to support their children's teachers. They were fighting side by side on issues both groups were passionate about: smaller classes, more resources for schools, over-testing, and racial equity.

The relationships started long before teachers walked out—even long before CORE members were elected. Chapter 3 told how CORE members worked alongside community groups like KOCO as far back as 2004, long before they had institutional power. "Working with the community was natural to us because we had already been working with the community," said Michael Brunson, now CTU's recording secretary.

More than just shoulder-to-shoulder activism, the union's ability to build enduring relationships came from its willingness to tackle the tough issues of race and class discrimination head-on and to listen to community members, not just work to get them on the union's message.

Katelyn Johnson, director of Action Now, a community organization active on the South and West Sides of the city, said her group had tried to work with the old CTU leadership "and found they weren't interested. If there was something they needed they would reach out, but after that you didn't hear from them." Botello said when the CORE members were elected, "it was like talking to organizers. The previous administration, they were politicians."

CTU Staff Coordinator Jackson Potter says the goal now is "a real relationship," one in which both union and community allies can "make mistakes and take risks to see where we can go and how far we can take it."

Community Board

Once in office, leaders wanted to formalize their relationships with community groups. They wanted to make sure there was always a channel for community and parent voices to be heard in the union.

So CTU established a new Community Board. At its nucleus were the organizations in the Grassroots Education Movement (GEM), which was born in 2008 to fight school closings (see Chapter 3). The groups were invited to a big rally against layoffs

Christa Lohman

and school closings, held in the Hyde Park/Kenwood area on the South Side in July 2010—the new leaders' first reach-out to the community.

Board members also came from the Grassroots Collaborative, a coalition formed by Service Employees (SEIU) locals and community organizations to campaign for a living wage ordinance for big-box stores (eventually vetoed by the mayor).

Mostly the groups on the Community Board had real membership roots in their neighborhoods, although a few were more of the think-tank variety. As in most large cities, plenty of nonprofit and neighborhood organizations existed that were content to attempt influence through back channels to politicians; these were not invited. CTU chose groups with organizing traditions and with attitudes toward the power brokers that matched CTU's new orientation.

"We gave more weight to groups that were more rooted in the community, rather than citywide organizations," said Organizing Director Norine Gutekanst, who worked closely with the Board. "We wanted people who really wanted to push on the school board, who identified their policies as racist. We chose organizations that believed that, rather than those who thought they could work with the school board."

According to Gutekanst, September and October 2010 were a "visioning period" for the Community Board, where the organizations discussed their top priorities in education, such as "social and emotional supports for children in the schools" (social workers and counselors), recruiting quality teachers from their own communities, and stopping the closings. "The visioning was a good way to all get on the same page," she said, "and for us to understand how the partner groups identified the problems with our schools."

The Board initially consisted of representatives from around 15 groups. (In 2012 it decided to re-adopt the name GEM. Today it includes 30 organizations and meets at least once a month.)

History teacher Jen Johnson pointed out that the Community Board rested on the years of work done by CORE before the slate was elected. "For CORE it was foundational to work with community groups to build a movement," she said. "We didn't want to just create a caucus. We wanted to create a movement, and we wanted people to buy in and to know we would not sell out if we were elected.

"CTU has tried to carry out the same vision. Having those community partners will help hold us accountable to that vision. They can help keep us on track."

Two Campaigns

After CPS CEO Ron Huberman stepped down in the fall of 2010, the union suggested a campaign for a say in choosing his replacement. Union and Community Board leaders chose a blue-ribbon panel of citizens to identify a schools chief with an education background—unlike Huberman and the two CEOs before him, whose backgrounds were in business.

And in 2012 groups on the Board launched a campaign for an elected, representative school board with seven of 13 spots reserved for parents. Since 1995 the mayor had controlled Chicago's schools through an appointed CEO and seven-member unelected board. These appointees tended to be wealthy businesspeople, not educators or working class parents. The lineup included Hyatt hotel heiress Penny Pritzker and banking executive David Vitale, ex-CEO of the Chicago Board of Trade. CTU developed a research paper on the value of elected boards.

A group called Communities Organized for Democracy in Education (CODE) was formed. Its tactic was to run nonbinding referendums in 327 precincts on the South and West Sides, to ask the state legislature to change the law that gave Chicago an appointed board. (Each precinct contains a couple thousand residents; there are 2,069 precincts altogether.) "They targeted wards and precincts that had been struck by a history of school closings and destabilization," Johnson explained.

Organizers presented 10,000 voter signatures in August to get the measure on the 2012 ballot in targeted precincts, and in November, a resounding 87 percent of those voting said yes. The victory was symbolic—actually switching to an elected board would require the state legislature to act—but the show of public support was a milestone.

Not surprisingly, neither of those campaigns directly moved Chicago's powers-that-be. Looking back, Potter had second thoughts about the union's push to engage the community in choosing the next CEO. It was "a good talking point, but that didn't translate into a campaign that had any chance of winning," he said. "It was too wonkish of an issue to get broad participation from the public. In hindsight it was a poor use of our time and energy."

The campaign for an elected board, on the other hand, worked out better—and this one had not been the CTU's idea, but came at the insistence of KOCO. "We were not sold on this being a good use of union resources, initially," Potter recalled, "because we were in the middle of a contract campaign." But KOCO correctly predicted how popular the idea would be, and pointed out that having no control over school governance made everything CTU did an uphill battle. Chicagoans could see that racism and class bias were the reasons city authorities had, as Potter put it, "a free pass to ignore the desires of their constituents."

The idea of an elected board was, and continues to be, "very easily supported everywhere we go," Gutekanst said. "It's a no-brainer: why would you have billionaires sitting on your school board? They don't have kids in our schools." Union leaders saw the elected board as a longer-term fight, something they knew they wouldn't win that year but could support with their contract campaign.

As it turned out, not many CTU members worked on the elected school board campaign personally, because they were

CTU

thoroughly involved in that contract campaign. But the two campaigns were complementary. "It helped to set the stage," said Gutekanst. "We could say, 'We're trying to get a better school day, but the school board is an obstacle.'" (See Chapter 7 on the "better school day" campaign.)

Gutekanst believes it's important that the Community Board "isn't a vehicle for CTU, it's a collaboration. Some things we agreed on that were joint campaigns, some not." Botello said, "We have some really honest and hard conversations. The union might say 'we can't weigh in as heavy as you-all.'" Johnson of Action Now says it's important to CTU's credibility with community groups that the union is also invested in issues that aren't directly tied to education, such as getting an ordinance requiring that vacant properties within a certain radius of schools must be boarded up and secured.

In addition to the Community Board, aided by the fact that one of CTU's in-house organizers is a minister, the union reached out to faith communities in the summer of 2011 to form Parents, Educators And Clergy for Education—PEACE. "Mayor Daley had certain ministers in his corner," Brunson explained. "Rahm Emanuel the same thing. We had a breakfast and a certain group came just to get information and report back to someone. So we drew back and formed a committee of clergy that we knew were aligned with our vision."

Local School Councils

Chicago schools differ from those in many other cities in that a voice for parents, community members, and teachers is built into school governance through the elected Local School Councils, which approve school budgets and hire the principal. In practice, the councils vary widely in their effectiveness. Some are rubber-stamps for the principal, some have low participation, and in the many schools on probation because of low test scores, their role is advisory only.

When CTU held its delegate training in March 2011, the invitation list was broadened to include the teacher reps on the LSCs. The union also obtained a citywide list of parent reps and sent them regular emails to keep them abreast of what was happening in the district and invite them to events.

In the strike, the LSCs didn't play a big role. It's easy to see their potential, though, if they were organized and strong. Fast-forward to summer 2013, when Rahm Emanuel announced drastic budget cuts, up to 25 percent for some schools. On the mostly middle-class North Side, some LSCs dared to defy the principal by voting down their diminished budgets. And as spring 2014 LSC elections neared, CTU planned a new emphasis that would encourage teachers to run, give training to those reps, and get active parents to run as well.

"We are really thinking through how we can get our members to deepen those relationships with parents," Gutekanst said.

From the beginning, the community partners shared the ideals that were animating CTU. "I remember an early meeting where they said, 'What is it that CTU is trying to do?'" says Gutekanst. "And I said, 'We're trying to build a movement in Chicago so that people in communities have some say-so in how the schools are run.'

"Heads nod, and they said, 'Let's build a movement.'"

✧

Read much more about CORE's and CTU's community alliances in Chapters 3, 7, 8, and 9.

Lessons

⇨ CTU saw alliances as year-round, not rustled up in an emergency.

⇨ CTU was upfront about its view that treatment of Chicago students amounted to institutional racism.

⇨ CTU was willing to take leadership from other groups, even if the union's own priorities were distinct.

⇨ CTU saw alliances as coalitions of equals that would learn from each other and sometimes agree to disagree or work separately.

⇨ CTU chose its allies carefully, declining to waste time on groups that were on a different page in their analysis of Chicago power politics.

⇨ CTU plans to use the Local School Councils, existing structures which have ranged from strong to moribund, and breathe new life into them through recruitment and training.

7

Fighting on All Fronts

The newly elected activists had ambitious plans to change course and make CTU a union that worked. And just as certain, district officials and Chicago's establishment had a plan to make sure they failed.

As the new leaders were sworn into office, the union faced another round of what Staff Coordinator Jackson Potter called "crisis budgeting" by the school board. In their first year they faced layoffs, anti-teacher legislation, another round of school closings, and the threat of a longer school day without fair compensation.

And leaders had to fight these attacks while they simultaneously began rebuilding CTU's strength from within (see Chapter 5).

What CTU leaders did not know was that Mayor Richard M. Daley was leaving city politics. His May 2011 replacement by Rahm Emanuel—later dubbed by the Occupy movement "Mayor 1%"—would mean an even fiercer attack on the schools and on teachers, with more closings, charters, and attempted pay cuts.

The union's battles produced mixed results in the new team's first two years. But these fights got members involved in their union and engaged with parents as never before. There could have been no better springboard into the contract campaign and strike.

Layoffs or Pay Cuts?

Just days after CORE won the run-off election in June 2010, the reformers called an emergency picket in front of the board of education. CEO Ron Huberman had announced the district was in financial distress. CTU must open the contract and give up all or part of members' 4 percent annual raise, Huberman said, or face as many as 2,000 layoffs.

Leaders didn't take Huberman at his word. CPS was offering no guarantees that, even if they did open the contract, members wouldn't be laid off anyway. "They weren't making some airtight commitment," said Debby Pope, now working in the Grievance Department. The district further pressed for a re-opener by presenting a list of options for the union "to pick and choose which things would add up to the savings they needed," said Financial Secretary Kristine Mayle.

"Our members were so insulted by this," Mayle said. "It was nickel-and-diming us on a whole bunch of little things"—including some permissive subjects, such as busing, that weren't in the contract.

To respond to CPS's proposal, leaders formed a broad bargaining team. They pulled in members to cover all grades, subject areas, regions, and ethnicities, and they reached out to activists beyond CORE, including members of opposing caucuses, with the aim of easing the election season polarization.

It was the first time CTU had brought members to the table along with officers and lawyers. "The board was very nervous about it," Mayle remembered, "and it helped add pressure on them because they had to face our members as human beings, with justified complaints—they weren't just numbers on a spreadsheet of potential layoffs."

The 30-person bargaining team got to see firsthand the cuts the district was proposing, and spread the word to others about the consequences. The union's message to rank-and-file teachers and the public, Mayle said, was, "however they were going to

CTU's 30-person bargaining team.

Solidarity

When Wisconsin teachers pulled a wildcat strike in February 2011 and occupied their state Capitol along with thousands of other workers, CTU jumped to offer solidarity to fellow teachers three hours away. Leaders knew it was a golden opportunity to educate members about the looming attacks on public employees and give them a feel for what a big struggle looks and feels like.

Three weekends in a row, CTU rented buses to take members up to Madison to show their solidarity with the crowds in the Capitol. For teachers who made the trip, witnessing the tens of thousands inside and surrounding the building was a big shot of adrenaline. "Members got a ton out of it," Kristine Mayle said of walking into the rotunda. "It was a good experience to feel that power."

The rebellion so close by was also "useful," said Jackson Potter, "to remind legislators in Illinois that, in the midst of their huge attack on our bargaining rights, this was going on in Wisconsin. If they went too far there could be an army of furious public employees and teachers breathing down their necks. It had the impact of moderating some of the attacks and giving us more time to prepare." ☼

squeeze out that money, it was going to be bad for the kids." CTU emphasized, "Losing teachers is bad for kids, too."

So leaders refused to open the contract, and instead demanded the district open its books. Nearly 1,300 teachers were laid off that summer. The union took the district to court over both the layoffs and the board's refusal to share public documents about CPS finances.

In October a judge ruled 750 of the layoffs illegal because Huberman had not used seniority to select those given pink slips. While this was a victory on paper, the district appealed, and the union knew the legal wrangling could drag out for months or years. (Indeed, state and federal courts both sided with the district when the case reached them in 2012.) The laid-off teachers were not brought back.

CTU leaders believed they were right not to take the bait and bargain against themselves. But it was also a lesson that judges and lawyers were not going to save Chicago's schools.

In September 2010 Mayor Daley announced he would not

seek another term. Huberman's resignation followed shortly. He was replaced by interim CEO Terry Mazany, followed by Emanuel's pick Jean-Claude Brizard.

Mayle said the constant changes in leadership "threw the whole system into chaos." Huberman had been interested in "data," but Brizard emphasized testing and a longer day: "It was constant upheaval. People didn't know what was expected of them anymore, and the people in charge didn't even know."

Legislating to Hamstring Teachers Unions

More attacks were coming, CTU leaders knew, besides the layoffs. Their former schools chief Arne Duncan was now head of Obama's Department of Education. One of his chief goals was to tie teacher evaluations to student test scores and thereby weaken seniority—and he was using the administration's $4.35 billion Race to the Top program as leverage (see the Appendix). Chicago teachers worried they would be the next target.

Traditionally, principals have evaluated teachers by observing their work in the classroom. But under the Race to the Top guidelines, in order to receive federal education grants, school districts and teachers unions must agree to use a "value-added model" that evaluates teachers by measuring students' improvement—or lack thereof—on standardized tests.

CTU leaders were concerned the value-added model would not show what teachers actually did, and would fail to factor in the outside influences on students: their home life, poverty, and unequal resources. Teachers labeled "ineffective" under the new model would be fast-tracked to dismissal. The effect was to put the burden on the teacher to turn things around—and blame her if she didn't.

Previous CTU leaders had agreed to let CPS use student performance as part of teacher evaluations, and had also agreed to cut pensions and introduce a two-tier pension system. But state leaders wanted bigger pension concessions from public sector workers. By January 2011, two bills in the state legislature threatened Chicago teachers along with all Illinois state workers.

The first was a pension "reform" bill, spearheaded by Democratic House Speaker Mike Madigan. The second was pushed by Advance Illinois and Stand for Children, a national nonprofit that was pressing legislation across the U.S. to weaken teachers' contract standards and expand charter schools. It aimed to limit bargaining rights and weaken tenure.

CTU and other state unions were able to fight off the pension attack. The education bill fizzled too, after a flurry of Capitol visits by CTU and both statewide teacher unions. They brought teachers, parents, and education groups to show legislators that disapproval was broader than just the union spokespeople.

But the union knew the billionaire-funded reformers would be back. After Stand for Children won a Colorado measure basing 50 percent of a teacher's evaluation on student test scores, the group wrote another Illinois bill: Senate Bill 7, introduced in spring 2011.

CTU President Karen Lewis joined the two statewide teacher unions to negotiate with legislators in the capital, Springfield. The state unions were prepared to make concessions—for example, to accept takeaways on seniority rights—in an attempt to keep even more draconian measures out of the bill.

Legislation in 1995 had already labeled certain vital topics as "permissive" subjects of bargaining for CPS, rather than mandatory. That meant management was not required to negotiate over class size, assignments, or school schedules, for example.

But SB7 went further, allowing CPS to make unilateral changes to teachers' working conditions that previously would have been negotiated. The district could now impose a longer school day and CTU could only bargain over the effects. Layoffs, previously based on seniority within the school unit, would now be based partly on evaluations, eroding seniority. Evaluations would determine whether teachers got tenure, and 25 percent of teachers' evaluations—rising to 30 percent after two years—would be based on student test scores.

The bill also set up roadblocks that Stand for Children leaders bragged would make it virtually impossible for Chicago teachers to strike. The new requirement—for Chicago teachers only—was that 75 percent of the entire bargaining unit, not just of those voting, would have to vote yes to authorize a strike.

In late-night negotiations in Springfield, with a Democratic senator shepherding the process, leaders of all three unions, including CTU, endorsed the bill.

Pushback

Lewis later said she'd felt she had limited options on SB7. "Our members were outraged by this—'why did you agree to this?'" she said. "I didn't have a choice—they were going to do it anyway."

And CTU was not alone. Many teachers union leaders across the country struggled during this period, as the anti-teacher, anti-union drumbeat intensified. Conservative politicians and their allies were threatening to go after all collective bargaining rights if unions didn't make concessions such as agreeing to limit tenure. In Massachusetts, for example, Stand for Children spearheaded a similar bill the next year—with bipartisan support in the legislature. The president of the main statewide teachers union there held closed-door talks with Stand for Children and legislators in an attempt at damage control. A public campaign against the measure, appealing to parents, was never considered.

Still, CORE members reacted strongly to the bill's endorsement by their own union. Several brought the question to the union's executive board. After discussion, Lewis was willing to back a resolution rescinding CTU's support. This was followed by a nearly unanimous vote of 600 members at the House of Delegates.

By that time, though, the measure had already sped through the Senate in a 59-0 vote. Soon after, it eased through the House as well, 112 to 1.

The incident could have been a black eye for CTU's new president and the local, and a source of mistrust in future union decision-making. But leaders' commitment to democracy enabled them to regroup and come back publicly with a unified position and a lesson learned: Don't let legislators isolate you in the pressure-cooker atmosphere of the capital. Insist on bringing big decisions back to the members.

Another lesson was that working with political leaders on their terms is a losing proposition. Democratic leaders, working with Stand for Children lobbyists, had set the parameters of the debate and created a false sense of urgency: the unions' endorse-

United Electrical Workers

Republic Windows and Doors workers occupied their factory in 2008, winning their demands and making a big impression on Chicago activists.

ment, they insisted, was needed *now!* CTU leaders decided that, while being involved in local and state politics was important, their strength would come from mobilizing their members and allies.

Going on Offense

The union now faced greater challenges than ever, with its sharpest weapon, a strike, seemingly yanked away. And in May 2011, Rahm Emanuel strutted into the mayor's office.

Emanuel had campaigned on fixing Chicago's school system. He praised charters and offered "tough choices" for traditional public schools. His remedy would be to lengthen the school day and order dozens of turnarounds. A well-connected charter school operator was a key Emanuel advisor on education issues.

So CTU leaders would have to not only defend members' contract but at the same time respond to a tidal wave of school closings and privatization. They would be bargaining with a district that was claiming a $700 million deficit. Merit pay, tenure, and seniority rights would be on the table.

As it happened, a December 2008 factory occupation at a Chicago window manufacturer had made a big impression on local activists. Faced with a sudden closing, workers at Republic

Windows and Doors held a sit-in to demand the pay they were owed. Union activists flocked to the West Side plant to support them. The workers not only won their demand but also captured national attention and sympathy, lifting the spirits of unionists across the country.

"Republic showed—you want to change the conversation, take action," said organizer Matthew Luskin.

So CTU set about changing the conversation by taking action. Instead of retreating and softening their messages and tactics, members went out and engaged with the public on terms set by the union.

By going on offense, CTU succeeded in making its members the good guys instead of the bad guys. The issue wasn't lazy teachers worrying about their retirement; it was years of neglect of schools in African American and Latino neighborhoods. The question wasn't just teacher layoffs but class size. And CTU turned its lens on what was causing these problems, educating everyone about how schools were getting short shrift while banks and corporations got tax breaks.

Money for Schools, Not Corporations

CTU tied its critique of school financing to the bigger economic forces that were hurting Chicago's working class residents. The union pointed the finger at corporations for profiting off school privatization and for robbing schools of much-needed resources.

CTU, Service Employees (SEIU) locals, and the Kenwood Oakland Community Organization (KOCO) joined forces in March 2011 to protest at a Cadillac dealership that had received $8 million from the city in TIF funding, the mayor's slush fund. Teachers and activists marched from a recently shuttered elementary school to the dealership and refused to leave. Potter and an activist from the disability rights community were arrested. The coalition demanded that the dealership return the funding to the city to be used for schools.

"Big business is taking resources away from schools and working families," Potter told the *Chicago Tribune*, "and we want it back immediately."

CTU

In June the union held a Saturday "grade-in" at three Bank of America locations in the Belmont-Cragin, Pilsen, and South Shore neighborhoods. Teachers graded papers in the bank lobbies—then on the sidewalks, after they got kicked out—to highlight their round-the-clock work. Bank of America and three other investment banks were draining $36 million a year from the school district budget in interest on "swaps" contracts, where the district paid a high fixed interest rate while the banks reaped profits from the

Education in a Different Classroom

CTU sent 38 members to a Labor Notes Troublemakers School held in Chicago in May 2011, where Karen Lewis spoke in a plenary called "We're All in This Together: Building Labor-Community Alliances."

Alongside other unionists and folks from worker centers such as Arise Chicago, the teachers heard from Madison teachers union President Peggy Coyne on "Lessons from Wisconsin" and went to workshops on contract campaigns, fighting discipline and dismissal, and "Rahmbo vs. the Unions."

Middle school teacher Kimberly Bowsky said she liked seeing unionists school each other. "Usually you learn organizing by just joining a group and doing it," she said. "Nobody teaches you." ✿

CTU

historically-low post-crash interest rates. The very banks whose behavior had fueled the financial crisis were now taking advantage of its aftermath to rip off cities.

"We were exposing how corporate tax loopholes were harming education and public schools," history teacher Jen Johnson explained. "It was important for us to say, 'If you didn't participate in selling debt, and if you didn't give tax breaks to corporations and banks, the district would have more money.'"

The union was an early partner in Stand Up Chicago, an SEIU-led coalition formed in the summer of 2011. Members included the United Electrical Workers and community groups like KOCO and Action Now.

Stand Up organizer Alex Han explained that the group came together to address economic justice issues not directly related to union contracts. It was part of a national SEIU campaign, Fight for a Fair Economy, which played out differently in different cities. In Chicago it had local ownership and grassroots participation, building on a lively committee that had come together to fight for a living wage ordinance for big-box stores.

One of Stand Up's main targets was TIF funds (see box). Its inaugural action was a June 2011 protest at a meeting of corporate finance executives at a downtown hotel. More than 3,000 people turned out, including 500 teachers. Protesters blocked the street and several CTU leaders were arrested demanding an end to the corporate welfare they said was stealing from Chicago families.

The intent was to redirect the political animosity aimed at public sector workers to focus instead on the real sources of the city's problems: the banks and the politicians like Emanuel who helped them dodge responsibility for the meltdown they'd caused.

"There was a lot of excitement after that," Han said. CTU invited school closing activists to feed into Stand Up's bigger, city-wide protests. Large-scale demonstrations and militant tactics involving arrests and disruption would become familiar by the time of the strike.

When the Occupy movement appeared in fall 2011, Stand Up and CTU seized the opportunity to hook up with new allies who agreed with their emphasis on inequality and who liked bold tactics. Stand Up launched an October week of action to coincide with the beginning of the Occupiers' downtown sit-in. The group protested at meetings of the Mortgage Bankers Association and the Futures Industry Association; 8,000 people clogged traffic around the meeting hotels. "How to fix the deficit? Tax, tax, tax the rich," they chanted.

Tiff over TIFs

Chicago's tax increment financing program (TIF) was intended to direct a portion of property tax dollars to blighted areas, rather than into the city's general budget. The idea was to capture funding for areas in need of development; the program sets aside up to $450 million annually.

In practice, though, TIFs became a slush fund for the mayor's pet projects, over the years generating more than a billion dollars outside the city budget that could be doled out to corporations and developers, even in parts of the city where it was dubious to claim blight. TIF money has been used to subsidize luxury housing and big-box retail stores, often passing through the hands of politically connected developers and big banks.

CTU and its partners argue that TIF money should go to fund desperately under-resourced schools. "There are over 100 schools that don't have stand-alone libraries because Chicago's elected officials are spending millions on political patronage and calling it economic development," said Jesse Sharkey, CTU vice president. ✿

CTU and SEIU members linked arms during a week of action led by Stand Up Chicago and Occupy in October 2011. Target: the banks.

The coalition blamed the banks for bringing on the financial crisis, then evicting families and leaving their vacant houses to fall into disrepair. They pointed out that foreclosures and evictions were draining cities of property taxes that could go to schools. Marchers dumped garbage from a neighborhood cleanup onto the floor of a downtown Bank of America.

As the Occupy movement continued, CTU reps attended weekly meetings of the Occupy labor committee and won the group over to the idea of concentrating on schools, rather than a laundry list of issues. They even hosted meetings at CTU headquarters. People in that group later became the nucleus of the Chicago Teachers Solidarity Committee during the strike.

In 2013 CTU would work with Occupiers again to protest school closings. Occupy activists, and union members, and community group leaders blocked elevators at City Hall in an act of civil disobedience, and were arrested.

The union was not afraid to work with allies deemed too radical for the mainstream. "A lot of teachers got arrested the night they cleared out the park," Mayle said, referring to the night Chicago police evicted the Occupy encampment. Occupiers who had no direct connection to Chicago schools were willing to come out when their ally asked. Said Potter, "Don't underestimate direct action, taking risks, taking chances. Don't underestimate the power of solidarity to get people to put themselves at risk."

By challenging the politicians who claimed the city was broke, CTU members created their own terms for a discussion of how public schools should be funded and run. They hit their stride as an organization, setting the stage for a different kind of contract bargaining, connected to a wide community-labor coalition.

Too Radical?

In the midst of the continuing political attacks on teachers, an important lesson for members worried about bad media coverage was that when CTU got good press, it was because the members *did* something. It was not a question of hiring media consultants; it was taking over the Cadillac dealer who got TIFs, holding a vigil at Emanuel's house against school closings, parents and teachers getting arrested together.

All these press moments were the result of rank-and-file members disrupting things for the schools' enemies and dramatizing what the fight was really about.

These actions were also crucial in changing the culture of the union. CTU had little tradition of militant rallies, civil disobedience, or aggressive actions. Many teachers are "rule followers" by nature, but through these events thousands got to see CTU activists pushing over police barricades, ignoring orders, being arrested, sitting in, shouting down politicians, and disrupting meetings—all on behalf of the students. These actions were typically done side by side with parents and community organizations, at a time when many members believed that the public blamed teachers for the schools' admitted problems.

Some within the union and in CORE were afraid these activities would go too far for the average member. They worried that militancy would alienate less active members who wanted to focus on their daily issues in the schools. Instead, the high-profile actions began to draw out new activists. Members could make the connection: challenging the mayor and his allies, while winning over parents and the public, would affect how aggressive principals could be in the buildings, too.

A Longer School Day

Rahm Emanuel had campaigned on the promise to institute a longer school day, and he took up that fight immediately after taking office. The union was still smarting from passage of SB7. The new law allowed the district to impose a longer school day or school year without negotiating with the union.

Emanuel framed the change as a no-brainer. The school day was five hours and 45 minutes in elementary schools, the shortest in the country. His push was to lengthen it to seven-and-a-half hours and extend the school year by 10 days. Teachers would get a 2 percent raise for 20 percent more work. Charter schools were already doing it; parents would be happy, Emanuel claimed. "It was Rahm's first shot at us," said Mayle.

In late August, when teachers were in the schools but students had not yet arrived, CPS convinced teachers at 13 schools to vote to waive the union contract and lengthen their day. "They bribed teachers with iPads and money for their schools and pushed principals to call waiver votes quickly," Mayle said. "The schools they got were those with young staff, with Teach For America staff, or schools without CTU delegates."

When the union's district supervisors (see Chapter 5) got wind of the waivers, they called union headquarters and "we sprung into action," said Organizing Director Norine Gutekanst, "to immediately get the message across to all the members that this was an illegal attempt by the board to go around the union that represents all of the teachers, and really they should not be falling for this."

"Our high schools were traditionally our strongest, most militant members," organizer Matthew Luskin remembered. Elementary teachers were quieter and were generally uncomfortable with the idea of reaching out to parents as union activists. When Emanuel called on parents to demand the longer day, "that's when charts went up on the wall tracking the status at every school: Is a vote happening? Will we win? Can we kill it off before that point? Did they already vote yes?"

Organizers called in staff from other departments and sched-

uled emergency union meetings at the schools, citywide. Members were asked to get all their co-workers on the same page, publicly take a position, and begin talking to parents.

"Scores of parent and Local School Council meetings were scheduled on the longer school day," said Luskin, "and this was often by parents or principals who were intending to push for the vote. Members had to choose to talk to those parents in a situation that could have been very hostile. Organizers were available to help people prepare, but only members from that school could effectively carry the message to their parents.

"At school after school it went great: Parents who started the meeting saying 'it would be crazy for our school to pass up this money' and urging teachers to vote yes ended it by saying 'this seems like that union-busting we saw in Wisconsin' and passing resolutions condemning the board for spending money trying to turn parents against teachers.

"It was a defining moment and an experience that helped elementary teachers across the city believe that the campaigns to come were possible."

Emanuel did not anticipate the resistance his proposal would face from parents. He ended up handing CTU the perfect issue to organize around. Teachers were outraged at the proposal to increase their work hours without a significant pay increase. And parents and teachers alike found it foolish to simply add time to an under-resourced school day without adding any new programs.

CORE member Adam Heenan said Emanuel was the union's best organizer. "He was openly hostile to the teachers union," Heenan said. "Now we were at the point of insults and a heavier workload."

Wendy Katten, a CPS parent and director of the parent group Raise Your Hand, said, "We were hearing that people weren't getting IEPs [Individualized Education Programs, mandated for children with disabilities] for their kids, that they don't have paint for art class in their schools. There are all these things that aren't being addressed right now. If we don't fix those things, how is more time going to help?"

Chicago Parents for Quality Education, a coalition of parent and community groups, agreed, saying that students could best be served by giving schools more resources and distributing them equally.

In October, CTU got a ruling from the Illinois Education Labor Relations Board. The board blocked CPS from soliciting additional schools to work more hours, because the district was bypassing the collective bargaining agent, the union. Meanwhile, public opinion had turned definitively against Emanuel's unilateral longer school day plan. It was the mayor who ended up bruised, not the union.

In April 2012 CTU publicized a report written by allies at the University of Illinois at Chicago: *Beyond the Classroom: An Analysis of a Chicago Public School Teacher's Actual Workday*. It found that Chicago teachers worked an average of 58 hours a week during the school year, dispelling the myth that a teacher's day ends at 3 p.m.

Union bargainers settled the longer school day in July 2012, as momentum was building towards a strike. The deal required el-

The latest scheme by right-wing school "reformers" is to lengthen the school day...

HUCK/KONOPACKI TEACHER CARTOONS
WWW.SOLIDARITY.COM/HKCARTOONS - AUG

KONOPACKI
©2012

ementary schools to increase their day by an hour and 15 minutes, to seven hours of school. Before, elementary teachers had had their "lunch" at the end of the day after students went home, and the teachers could leave, too. With the new schedule, the teachers' one-hour lunch was moved to during the day. High schools added 30 more minutes, and 10 days were added to the school calendar.

But each teacher's actual work day was not lengthened significantly, because CPS agreed to hire 512 more teachers, nearly one per school. The new hires were to come from the pool of teachers laid off the previous fall and be specialists in music, library science, languages, art, and other "enrichment" areas.

While both sides declared victory, the fact was that CTU leaders had forced the district to negotiate over what state law said was off limits.

The fight on the longer school day provided "excellent practice for the contract campaign," Mayle said: marshaling arguments, getting parents on the union's side, and holding firm at the bargaining table. And as the contract campaign grew during 2012, the school day fight dovetailed with it, shifting public opinion to favor the teachers on the very issues teachers unions had been losing on nationally—and proving it was possible to reframe the conversation.

Anticipating School Closings

About 100 public schools had been shuttered since the Renaissance 2010 school privatization plan began in 2004. In their place were 85 charter schools with a mostly non-union workforce.

Rather than take the attitude that the union's job was to cut its losses and manage the decline of public schools, leaders determined to fight all the closings and resist attempts to pit schools against each other.

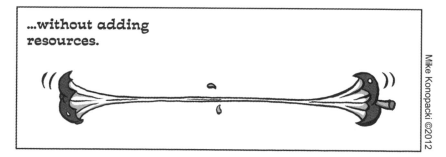

...without adding resources.

Mike Konopacki ©2012

Sarah Jane Rhee, loveandstrugglephotos.com

Parents and teachers held a vigil to protect "La Casita," a building at Whittier Elementary School that CPS wanted to demolish, October 2010.

Every fall the board voted on which criteria to use for closing schools. So in fall 2011, the CTU Research Department looked at all the criteria and metrics, to predict which schools might be targets. This way the union could have organizing conversations with teachers and community partners ahead of time. "We sent organizers and field staff out to schools ahead of the deadline," said Gutekanst. "People knew this was on the horizon and the union was going to be actively opposing it."

CORE had managed to fight off some of the closings in earlier years (see Chapters 3 and 4). In the 2008-09 school year, 22 closings were announced; after campaigns and protest, the board reduced the number to 16. In 2009-10, the board announced 14 shutdowns, and community, parents, and teachers again succeeded in fighting off six.

Mazany's hit list in 2010-2011 was even shorter—and the activists saved two. It was becoming clear the school closures and consolidations were far from inevitable. A well-organized group could beat them, and more and more people across the city were learning how. In 2011-12 the union called for a citywide moratorium on closings.

"I remember thinking we had to step it up," said elementary teacher Al Ramirez. The previous CTU administration had claimed to offer members ways to get involved, but had not had a serious organizing plan. He recalled hearings where teachers and parents had participated only passively, waiting in line to speak for two minutes and then leaving.

Leaders had to create a new sense of urgency. The shift was evident, Gutekanst said, in how CTU organizers talked about closings with teachers. "We said, 'If your school is not on the list, we want you to come support all the schools that will be on the list.'"

Ramirez described the strategy: "Let's not make these changes easy for the very rich. Let's embarrass them at every point we can. Let's expose them at every place we can and make it difficult for them publicly."

Getting teachers involved in fighting the closings, the longer day, and charter school expansion (often all at the same time) was not automatic. Emanuel was riding high; it looked like the newly victorious mayor would be able to get whatever he wanted.

But CTU leaders went back to fundamentals. Organizers, staff, and elected representatives started calling school meetings with two goals: letting teachers articulate their concerns, and giving them a credible plan to fight back.

Teachers first had space to vent their frustrations about how their students and their schools were being treated. Organizer Brandon Johnson described this part of the meeting as "listening to people express their anger and making sure their anger was directed at the right enemy." Organizers' job was to make sure members' sights were raised beyond contract issues to the power dynamics in Chicago, to understand that a powerful elite was making the decisions about public education.

The second objective was sharing a plan to fight. This included gathering local input on how to execute the plan. "We have a general strategy and then the organizers adapt," said longtime CORE member Debby Pope. "There is no one-size-fits-all."

"Most folks thought it would be difficult to win in this environment," said Johnson—in an understatement. He put it to them in stark terms: "The profession that we love is under attack. The only way we can defend it is by sticking together. We are all we have at this point."

Bridging the Disconnect

Herzl Elementary is a good example of CTU's back to basics approach. The school was slated for turnaround, and the teachers hadn't been very involved in union activities up to that point.

Parents Occupy a School

The occupation of Piccolo Elementary School was one example of what Jitu Brown described as "the most militant response that Chicago has ever had" around education, in the year leading up to the strike.

Parent activists with the group Blocks Together occupied Piccolo in February 2012 to protest a private takeover in which the entire staff would be fired. Teachers came out in support.

CPS had targeted the West Side school, which served 550 mostly black and Latino students, to reopen under the privately managed Academy for Urban School Leadership (AUSL), known for pushing out students considered problem children.

'Bring Them to Us'

Parents voted overwhelmingly against privatizing the school and developed their own counter-proposal. The plan included keeping the new principal for a minimum of two years, increasing parent engagement, and funding more cultural programs and better security.

Latrice Watkins, chair of the Local School Council, ticked off improvements that had already happened: better attendance, a more respectful culture, a more responsive principal, parents involved in hallway patrols and invited into the classrooms, and better parent-teacher communication.

"We do not want AUSL to come to our school," Watkins said, "because we are already doing our own turnaround."

Piccolo parent Latoya Walls pushed for the occupation. "They're used to having rallies in front of downtown, just another thing going on," Walls said. "I said 'No, bring them to us, and

Sarah Jane Rhee, loveandstrugglephotos.com

let's occupy this building.' I didn't know it was going to turn out to be this big."

Parents, teachers, students, and Occupy Chicago members linked arms on the school's front steps singing "Ain't Gonna Let Nobody Turn Me Around." The square in front was filled with tents for a planned encampment, and signs declared "We Do Not Need AUSL."

They occupied the school for nearly 24 hours, winning citywide attention and leaving the building only after board leaders promised meetings with parents. Nevertheless, the meetings—mostly conducted by conference call the following week—didn't stop the board from going forward with the turnaround of Piccolo. ✿

Their school had gone through a number of administrators, the building was in disrepair, and many felt it was being intentionally starved so the district could justify drastic action.

An organizer contacted the delegate first, asking to set up a meeting to talk about conditions at the school. Rather than announcing "a march, a phonebank, or fill up a bus," Johnson said, the approach was, "Here's what's going on, you guys have heard the news—what do you feel like doing?"

When teachers met, they talked about how the schools had been set up to fail and how they felt neglected. At first they asked what the union was going to do, as if it were a third party. But the question was directed back at those in the room: what are *we* going to do?

"There was a disconnect; parents and teachers hadn't worked together," Johnson said. "We actually are fighting hard; we are just not fighting together."

So the teachers began coordinating their efforts with West Side community groups. They phonebanked parents about getting involved. And they filled two buses to go to the closure hearings, where many teachers gave compelling testimony.

The Closings Plan

On December 1, 2011, Emanuel proposed seven school closings and phase-outs, 10 "turnarounds" in which all the teachers and staff would be fired, and six "co-locations," where private charter school operators would grab portions of existing public schools. All 23 schools were on Chicago's predominantly black and Latino South and West sides.

Two days later, CTU and the Community Board responded with a teach-in that brought 500 to a high school on the South Side. The atmosphere was militant. One participant told the crowd, "I have been through four—count them, four—closings and turn-arounds. And I want you to know that I have beat them each and every time." Angela Surney, who helped fight off the shuttering of her son's Marconi Elementary, got a standing ovation when she explained how to be a "victor" rather than a "victim."

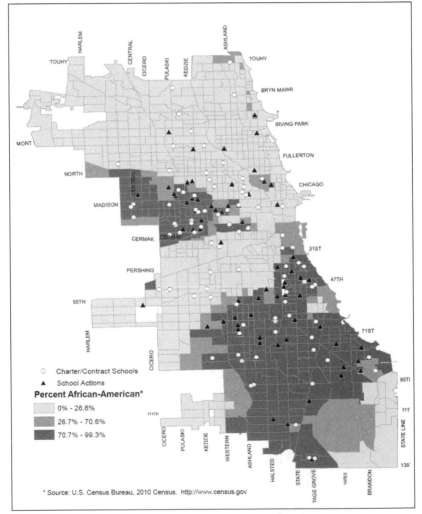

A map from CTU's 2012 report *The Black and White of Education in Chicago's Public Schools* highlights how a decade of disruptive school actions (closings, phase-outs, and turnarounds) and incursions by charter schools disproportionately targeted the city's African American neighborhoods.

T.B. Furman

KOCO organizer Jitu Brown noted that many schools now targeted for closure because of poor test scores had been destabilized when they started receiving students ousted from other closed schools. A representative from the Brighton Park Neighborhood Council pledged her group's turnout at school board actions and offered Brighton Park's community schools—which stayed open late providing a range of services—as a positive example. Other participants promised to bring busloads of parents to vigil at the school board.

Even teachers not directly threatened showed up; 90 schools were represented.

More meetings were held around the city, organized on the basis of CPS's geographical "network" areas. In the Midway Network, for example, 60 teachers and community members from 16 schools across a swath of the Southwest Side planned a Martin Luther King Day march to save a 1,400-student K-8 school.

Opposing Educational Apartheid

As CTU fought the closings, their disparate effect on students of color, especially black students, was one of the union's main battle cries. Leaders called the board's policies racist, pointing out that since 2001, 88 percent of students affected by closings and turnarounds had been African American.

Brandon Johnson and other black CTU leaders appeared regularly on the major black talk-radio station to raise this issue. By systematically depriving black and Latino communities of resources, CTU said, CPS was setting schools up to fail. Tammie Vinson, the delegate at Emmet Elementary, said, "All these assessments are rating our schools as failing, our teachers as failing, our students as failing. Everybody's failing based on these assessments."

Lewis described Chicago as entering an "era of educational apartheid."

Black teachers were also the most affected by the closings, as they were more likely to teach in the heavily black schools. In February 2012 CTU and four teachers filed a complaint with the Equal Employment Opportunity Commission, alleging that the board's layoff policy "had a systemic, class-wide, disparate impact on African American teachers," Lewis said. (CORE had in 2009 filed an EEOC complaint on a similar topic. See Chapter 3.)

In support of its charge, the union noted that in the 2011 school year, 29 percent of CPS's tenured teachers were African American—but blacks were 43 percent of those affected by that year's layoffs.

(It got worse. In a January 2013 op ed, Johnson wrote, "In 2000…41 percent of CPS teachers were black. Today…just 25 percent of teachers are black.")

To ameliorate the losses, CTU would fight for contract language to help teachers follow their students when schools closed, and even got the board to agree to recruit a racially diverse workforce (see Chapter 10).

CTU's new honesty on the fraught subject of race won it many allies, not only in the communities but within the union's own ranks. "The emergence of CORE allowed many of us African Americans to go, 'This is something we can get with,'" said middle school teacher Kimberly Bowsky, who joined CORE after the caucus took office.

Jen Johnson cites outreach to black churches, relationships with PUSH (the Jesse Jackson organization), and Karen Lewis's own "cachet as an individual." For decades the black South Side has sponsored a "back to school" parade every August, with bands and kids doing gymnastics. "I think CTU always participated but in the last few years it has grown tremendously," Johnson said. "We have a float, Karen sits on it, we're out in our red shirts."

Any politician can ride a float, but CTU had made it clear in word and deed that fighting educational apartheid was the heart of the union's mission.

Save Our Schools

As CTU and the Community Board carried out their proactive agenda across the city, the atmosphere began to change.

The tactics of the union-community coalition were confrontational, and they escalated. Coalition members disrupted and took over a school board meeting, chanting and leading their own meeting after board members fled. Parents and community activists occupied schools. The Community Board led a five-day sit-in at City Hall in January 2012; 200 people showed up, but the mayor still refused to meet to discuss school closures.

In every action, CTU stressed the big picture. These visible examples of joint union-community action built teachers' and community members' confidence in the types of tactics that would later be used during the strike.

Five hundred people vigiled by candlelight at the mayor's house to challenge the closure plans—an effort led by community groups, with CTU following their lead. On the day the board was to vote, hundreds of parents, students, teachers, and community members showed up at dawn to get on the speakers' list.

The fight was brutal, and in the end the board voted to approve almost all the proposed closures and other actions.

Emanuel had won that round. But the union and parents could point to communities newly mobilized to support a vision of education that addressed poverty and racism. The actions had cemented support for the teachers—while Emanuel and the board had demonstrated they weren't interested in anything parents had to say. The networks and methods used to educate and turn out members and allies would overlap with CTU's work gearing up for the contract campaign.

CTU's Agenda for the Schools

As all these battles raged, "we started talking about the need for us to have a positive program. We couldn't just be against,

The Schools Chicago's Students Deserve

CTU's report laid bare the ugly under-resourcing of Chicago schools, made recommendations for what students needed—backed up with research findings—and suggested where the money could come from.

The union argued that students needed nurses and social workers to help them deal with health issues like asthma, hearing and vision problems, lack of food, and the daily traumas some faced. Only 202 nurses and 370 social workers were serving 684 schools.

Noting that 160 elementary schools had no library, the union called for library/media instruction, physical education, arts education (music, drama, art, dance, choir, band), science laboratories, and computer science.

Chicago's class-size guidelines suggested a 28-student cap for lower grades and 31 in middle school, but these guidelines were often violated, with up to 40 in a classroom. CTU cited research that showed students would perform better with 13-17 students per class, particularly in lower grades.

The report tied members' job security to students' well-being, calling for "a diverse—and stable—workforce of teachers and paraprofessionals to provide a secure environment."

And CTU told Chicagoans where the money to fund such excellent schools could be found: from TIF money, from progressive taxation, and through an end to corporate tax loopholes and subsidies.

The report is at bit.ly/SchoolsDeserve. ✿

against, against; we needed to be for something," said Carol Caref, now head of the CTU Research Department.

Thus was born *The Schools Chicago's Students Deserve*, advocating a "better school day" rather than merely a longer one. The 46-page February 2012 report, the fruit of months of meetings and exchanges, became the union's signature public statement on what education in Chicago should look like, a point-by-point synopsis of exactly what the union was fighting for.

"The CTU Community Board had been pushing for this, so they were very involved," Caref said. Board members added emphasis on the need to engage parents in the plans for schools. Activists from PURE, a citywide parent group, and VOYCE, a youth organization, wrote sections.

"I don't believe in this garbage they keep saying about us only thinking about ourselves," explained Bowsky. "Class size is an imperative: to have a ratio of children that's reasonable for one adult to spend time with and pay attention to.

"To tell parents, teachers, and students that we have to raise class size simply because of money, that we can't afford it—well, the bosses who make these decisions never tell themselves that. Their kids have space."

The report was circulated to allies, given to state representatives and aldermen, and pushed to the media. Teacher activists took copies to every meeting they went to. Brandon Johnson said parents saw the report as a breath of fresh air. "People were very much relieved that you actually had a document that articulated their desires," he said. "Someone is actually talking about poverty, talking about enriched curriculum. It was a guide to what we were fighting for."

Lessons

⇨ As CTU leaders made plans to rebuild their union, they were acutely aware that management had its own plan. They educated themselves and the members on all aspects of "education reform" (see Appendix) and on city financing so they would not be caught off-guard by management.

⇨ Early on, the new leaders brought former opponents onto the bargaining team to avoid unnecessary divisions, and to build a representative committee.

⇨ CTU leaders refused to give up what members were legally owed (including a contractual pay raise) in exchange for non-binding promises. They didn't let themselves be drawn into CPS's game of "how much will you give up to save the kids?" which would have meant teachers accepting the blame for the state of the schools.

⇨ CTU didn't try to manage the downsizing of the schools but instead opposed it entirely. The union played offense instead of defense, refusing to accept what its enemies called "reality."

⇨ The union offered proactive solutions to improve schools. It researched and published its own well-thought-out plan for Chicago schools, aiming high and explaining where the money could be found.

⇨ CTU named the enemies: the 1%, inequality, a billionaire-funded drive to defund and privatize public education—and in particular, institutional racism, which they labeled educational apartheid. By doing so, they educated many and made allies of those who already were well aware of the racism in the school system.

⇨ CTU learned that playing by politicians' rules is lose-lose. Leaders determined not to accept the terms dictated by Democratic legislators, and instead to bring big decisions back to the union's elected body.

⇨ Democracy worked. The after-the-fact rejection of CTU's SB7 endorsement didn't sidetrack or weaken the union. Instead, the democratic practice steadied it for bigger fights ahead and got CORE caucus members more engaged.

⇨ CTU and its community partners planned and strategized together as equals. They used escalating tactics that were based on what grassroots groups wanted to do.

⇨ In the "better school day" campaign, CTU didn't accept the legal limits on mandatory subjects of bargaining. With their allies, they built a campaign that made the mayor bargain despite the rules.

⇨ CTU quickly recognized its common ground with Stand Up Chicago and Occupy Chicago, new groups taking bold actions and raising big-picture economic justice issues. The union allied itself with these groups and drew the connections to its own fight, winning allies that would provide key support for the strike.

⇨ Rather than being "too busy," CTU took advantage of opportunities to show solidarity, opening members' eyes to others' struggles, as in Wisconsin, Stand Up Chicago, and Occupy.

8

Contract Campaign

CTU's new leaders had begun laying the groundwork for a contract campaign and possible strike the moment they took office in 2010, two years out from contract expiration. They spent their first year in office breathing new life into the union's structures and briefing shop floor leaders on what it would take to put up a real contract fight (see Chapter 5).

But as their second school year began in fall 2011, they had to shift that organizing into higher gear and begin the contract campaign in earnest. By June 2012, the union would need to win a strike vote—and be ready to follow through.

Illinois legislators had set CTU an even higher bar than most unions face—75 percent of the full membership would have to vote yes to authorize a strike—but the basic principles were the same as in any contract fight. They did it with good old-fashioned organizing.

This meant thousands and thousands of one-on-one conversations between leaders in the schools and their co-workers. It meant charts on the union office wall to keep track of every school and every delegate. It meant that, in each school, organizers assessed, re-assessed, and re-re-assessed their support. And "organizers" meant not just the Organizing Department staff but district supervisors and delegates, too.

"We did a lot of counting," Organizing Director Norine Gutekanst said later. All those counts were laying the groundwork for the big one in June, when CTU would proudly count to 23,780—90 percent of its members—voting yes for a strike.

At the same time, there were plenty of strategy discussions, not just among officers and staff but with the members. "People weren't promised a victory if we struck," remembered organizer

Matthew Luskin, "just that we would have a chance. We were brutally honest that a strike could lose, certainly wouldn't be enough by itself, and that even with a victory it would only be partial."

Forming the Contract Action Committees

How to structure a member-to-member network is something unions have pretty well figured out. The lingo varies from union to union, but the idea is the same: a phone-tree-like structure, where each Contract Action Committee member is responsible for staying in regular touch with about 10 fellow employees.

One person per school, often a delegate, would be the Contract Action Committee head, in touch with all committee members in her building. Each committee member's 10 contacts might include not only teachers and paraprofessionals in CTU but also staff represented by other unions, such as custodians, lunchroom workers, and special education classroom assistants.

Equally important was communication with parents. Members were asked to reach out to supportive parents and organize a discussion about the issues that had brought them to the point of supporting a strike.

CTU's district supervisors formed a next layer of leadership. Each would be responsible for keeping in touch with all the Contract Action Committee heads in her geographic group. Once a month, each DS would call all the delegates in her group to pass on the latest talking points and requests from the union and find out how things were going. This "ongoing monthly personal relationship" between the DS and the delegate, said Gutekanst, became a key element of the campaign.

Where did committee members come from? Certainly not all were members of the CORE caucus—in fact, some had been active in rival caucuses. Union leaders wanted to draw a wide swath of members into action. Many were recruited from among the attendees at trainings, where the invitations were widened to include other activists as well as delegates.

Beyond that, CTU was holding lots of after-school outreach events around the city: inviting members to come ask questions and hear from officers or organizers about the contract fight and ongoing issues. Email invitations went out to all members in a given area of the city. The union also held similar meetings school

Delegates are trained for action.

by school, targeting schools that had no volunteers yet for their action committees. "Every event we went to," Gutekanst said, "we
were always trying to sign people up to be part of the contract
action team."

Organizers sought to recruit those most respected and trusted by co-workers, and those who would represent the racial and
job-title diversity in each building.

Of course, activists adapted this model to the realities at their
own schools. At Seward Academy, where the delegate was pretty
inactive and many people were reticent about getting involved or
"didn't believe in unionism at all," language arts teacher Kimberly
Bowsky said, "everything we did was educating, right? We were
educating people who didn't know about unionism. So we didn't
break off into a Contract Action Committee. Everybody who
showed up at the union meeting was the committee."

Seward went from never having union meetings to having
them once a month. These meetings were "a process of constantly trying to move the delegate, talk about people's fears, and get
across that we are the union—to move from the mindset that 'I
pay my dues someplace down in the office,'" Bowsky said.

"We had to move people. There were people who thought, 'I
don't want to work next to that teacher, that teacher doesn't know

what they're doing.' We had to prove to our own members that we were in a context, that these were not issues of competence but issues of power, issues of the economy.

"It also helped that the mayor kept opening his mouth."

At schools threatened with closure, the fight against that and the contract campaign were one and the same. Educators at Emmet Elementary—mostly veterans of 25 years or more, high on the pay scale—recognized what a likely target their school was. "We understood they were probably going to close Emmet," said delegate Tammie Vinson. "So wearing red and showing solidarity was not a hard sell.

"The conversations were, 'Don't believe you can go in your classroom, close the door, and everything is going to pass by you,'" she said. "It's better to be a part of something, be vocal... Our plan was as a union to let people know that we're in it together."

Testing the Network

Starting in late 2011, committee members began circulating an open letter for teachers and parents to sign—showing their support for a rich curriculum, art instruction, recess, technology, quality lunches, functional heating and cooling systems, more social workers, counselors, and literacy staff, and after-school programs—as part of the fight over the longer school day. (For more on this fight, see Chapter 7.) There were versions in English and Spanish.

Taking the letter around gave members a chance to practice their organizing skills, while boosting their confidence at talking to parents about school problems. It was also the first test of the new organizing network.

By this time delegates were also spreading the word that union supporters should wear red every Friday—an informal way to warm people up for bigger mobilizing, and also to assess how far the network of support had reached thus far.

The genius of the "wear red" tactic is its simplicity. It's something concrete and low-risk that a delegate can ask anyone to do, even someone who has no extra time to be involved. The visibility helped alleviate fears, as co-workers who were on the fence could see for themselves the growing level of union support.

At first, many people would just wear a red scarf or a red-patterned blouse on Fridays—but as excitement and confidence grew, more and more ordered red CTU T-shirts. The union started selling them at the monthly House of Delegates meetings. "People would come in with orders for their whole school," recalled Debby Pope, now in CTU's Grievance Department.

The tactic "started causing a little bit of a stir," Pope said. Administrators noticed. Students noticed. Members loved it. Many sent in group photos of themselves and others at their schools, all in red, for the CTU website. At the height of the campaign, Staff Coordinator Jackson Potter estimates, 90 percent of schools had a significant number of members wearing red on Fridays. "This small, simple tactic built unity very quickly," said labor educator Steven Ashby, who helped train CTU members for the contract campaign. "It really invigorates people."

For citywide paraprofessionals like Charlotte Sanders, getting people to wear the red union T-shirts was "a big challenge" at first, because they didn't get to see others in their cohort wearing them. Sanders doesn't work at just one school; she travels from one to another, working alongside a social worker.

But that challenge turned out to be an organizing opportunity for her. "On Thursday I would send a text and say, 'Tomorrow is spirit day,'" she said. "I made personal phone calls, which was good because I could touch base about how their week went. Before the May 23 rally I was like, 'Everybody needs a shirt.'"

Sarah Jane Rhee, loveandstrugglephotos.com

CTU members marched downtown two weeks before their strike vote.

Of course, while some schools were solid red on Fridays, others were not. Some particularly intimidating principals would even announce that Friday was school spirit day, obliging teachers to wear school shirts. But this too was helpful information to gather. The district supervisor's role was to check in with the leaders at each school and find out: Were people wearing red? Were they signing the open letter? What roadblocks were committee members running into?

Training at the March 2012 delegate conference was crucial. Delegates and Contract Action Committee members went through the lists of members at their schools name by name—assessing whether each person was wearing red, would come to an action, and would vote yes for strike authorization.

Luskin remembers, "We focused on mapping and assessing your entire building, with the message that assessments are moving targets and the job of the delegate was to have a plan on how to *move* people. We offered them skills about how to overcome obstacles. It was empowering to people to realize that they could build support with these skills, rather than just lament the places it was missing."

Developing Demands

CTU had 28 longstanding member committees on areas such as early childhood education, substitutes, special education, and testing. Each issue committee came up with bargaining demands.

Other members weighed in at after-school meetings held around the city. Leaders pursued every opportunity to engage as many members as they could.

Curtis Elementary had six Contract Action Committee members who met to talk through the contract in detail: "What do you want to improve? What do you hate that's in there now that we could get out?" said Andrea Parker, the delegate and district supervisor. "The third grade teacher would talk to other third grade teachers, then we'd come back together and discuss." She brought the results of these conversations to delegate meetings or emailed them to union headquarters.

Some meetings were for specific groups, to make sure their particular needs didn't fall through the cracks. Paraprofessionals, for example, are educators who assist classroom teachers or provide specialized instruction themselves. It often happens that teachers unions focus only on teachers, leaving other members feeling alienated; Chicago was no exception. Many paraprofessionals felt disillusioned and disconnected from the union, Financial Secretary Kristine Mayle recalled.

So CTU's new leaders paid particular attention to the paraprofessionals, meeting with them by job category. Even the speech-language paraprofessionals—there were just eight of them citywide—had their own meeting and came up with their list of demands. Citywide paraprofessionals like Sanders were concerned about travel time. "If you have a school on the South Side and have to travel to the North Side, you get nowhere fast," Sanders explained—but the board was allowing just a 15- to 20-minute window, and wanted workers to travel on their lunch breaks, too. (The union won on this item, keeping a travel time limit out of the contract.)

After every group had submitted its demands, the proposals were finalized by the citywide Professional Problems Committee. This body is made up of committee chairs representing different subject areas and grades: the elementary committee, for example, and the social worker committee. The meetings were small at first, Mayle said, but grew to 25 or 30 per meeting "when they realized we were listening."

The PPC and union officers spent a month sorting through some 500 proposals from the various member committees and meetings. They weeded out those that seemed unworkable—but deliberately kept in a few that seemed "pie in the sky," Mayle said, such as a color printer for every teacher.

A key goal was to ensure that the union's proposals reflected its vision for public education. Members were proud that their proposals represented "the schools students deserve" (even if they would not win them all), in stark contrast to the board's proposals.

Equally important was to make sure the final list included an achievable goal for each subset of the membership—important for fairness, and also to cement everyone's support for a strike.

Mayle felt the union came close to achieving this goal. For social workers, school psychologists, and occupational, speech, and physical therapists, for example, CTU proposed and won the guarantee of a private space to work with students, including a computer with internet access and a locking file cabinet.

Phonebanking

In the past the union had relied heavily on member phonebanking for political candidates or about legislation, but often the phonebanking was seen as a way for officers to reward loyal supporters with a stipend for making the calls. The new leaders turned phonebanking into a way to have in-depth conversations with members.

"The heart of our trainings," said Luskin, "was to keep people from treating these like calls to get someone out to an event and instead to make sure it was about learning member concerns, along with discussion about strategy to win. We wanted to make sure that younger members were in dialogue with the union activists, that we were listening to what issues were important to them, what they were willing to fight for, what fears they had."

In the year before contract expiration, the phonebanking focused especially on calling new members, those who'd been working in the district for three years or less. New members would often be the least involved with the union and, as the lowest paid and least protected, they were the most vulnerable—and likely the most scared to take action. The phonebanking also focused on members at turnaround schools, paraprofessionals, clinicians who moved from school to school, and schools where there was no delegate.

"I think we would have been in trouble if we hadn't spent that time interacting with the young teachers," said special education teacher Margo Murray, who participated in many phonebanks.

These were in-depth conversations. Members trained by the Organizing Department (sometimes volunteering, other times paid) described the school board's and the mayor's bargaining goals, heard members' thoughts, and projected a vision of how the union could win. Members were asked to do something— come to a rally, attend a training, get involved in their school's contract committee or parent outreach, or fill buses to the state capital. (For more on the content of an organizing conversation, see Chapter 5.) Callers also advised members to save money in their own "strike funds," in case of a strike.

"At first the response was, 'I'm not going on strike, I have all these student loans, I can't afford to spend any time out of work,'" Murray said. "I would say, 'Can you afford to spend time *in* work if they end up destroying our contract?' I talked about the things they wanted to take away from us, and one of the biggest things was lanes and steps [which gave higher pay for more education, see Chapter 10]. 'If they take that away you'll get no credit in your pay for getting that expensive degree.'

"I went into the history: what happens when unions have to go up against management and we end up being divided instead of united," she said. "The conversation usually lasted 20 or 30 minutes. By that time they were extremely receptive."

Of course, as well as an education and mobilization tool, the calls were a way of counting noses: the caller tracked how willing the member was to vote for a strike. Winning a strike vote would require methods like this to objectively assess where members really were, not just where leaders hoped they were, so the union could see where to concentrate efforts.

CTU found ways to constantly reassess its support and test its ability to mobilize, throughout the contract campaign and even during the strike. Early tests were softer—participating in red-shirt Fridays, signing onto the open letter—but as the campaign intensified, the requests of members would intensify, too: casting a practice vote for a strike, coming out to a rally, casting a real vote for a strike, informational picketing. And every day during the strike, member leaders would count turnout at the picket lines. At any given moment, the power of the union depended on how many people it could mobilize into action.

Bargaining Team

The new leaders had had to convene a bargaining team right away after they took office in 2010, in order to bargain over lay-offs. They appointed 30 members drawn from all sectors, seniority ranges, and job categories, including executive board members but also the best leaders from other caucuses, a move designed to create buy-in and cooperation.

The team for the contract bargaining was a similar crew of 30 members and 15 alternates. Many members carried over from 2010. Some who'd become union staff had to be replaced, and the union again added members to make sure the team was a representative group and all bases were covered.

A smaller group formed the main team and did most of the talking in bargaining: the union's four officers, two lawyers, and staff coordinator. It was hard for the overburdened rank and filers on the team to make it to many bargaining sessions—especially during the school year—and there were an absurd number of sessions. Negotiations began in November 2011; the two sides entered mediation in February 2012. By the time the union gave strike notice in August, there had been almost 50 sessions.

So the small team did a lot of the day-to-day bargaining, but they wouldn't sign any tentative agreements until they had the approval of the "big bargaining team"—which they'd pull together for consultation every week or two.

If the team was divided about an issue, members would take it back to their schools to find out what co-workers thought. That is how they decided to accept management's proposal to end deferred pay, for instance. (Starting in fall 2013, teachers are paid only during the school year. Under the old system, some of their pay would be held back and paid out over the summer. The total annual pay was the same.)

They found that while, under the old system, members liked the convenience of not having to save during the year, they also mistrusted the CPS payroll department, which had a habit of messing up. Some members felt that rather than loan the district money—while it held the pay and collected interest—they could

A Former Rival on the Bargaining Team

Math teacher Keith Vandermeulen ran for financial secretary on the incumbent UPC ticket in 2010, losing to Kristine Mayle. Nonetheless, he stayed active in the union and became a member of the "big bargaining team."

In a June 2012 article for the union's website, Vandermeulen bluntly characterized himself as a former political rival but praised the inclusive approach the new officers had introduced. "The process has been democratic but well organized by the table team," he wrote. "Union leadership has acted on many recommendations given by rank-and-file members."

The diversity of rank-and-file voices on the bargaining team, he predicted, would produce a better contract in the end. ✿

be trusted to manage their own money. "The members started out divided, but ultimately distrust of CPS's handling of our payroll won out," Mayle said.

During bargaining, team members passed notes to President Karen Lewis if they had a question, or if they heard district bargainers say something they knew wasn't true at their school. Lewis might ask the question herself, or call the member to the table to speak directly to the board.

"I'm very pleased to see how much clinicians are able to speak at the meetings, because we are neither fish nor fowl—we're not teachers, we're not PSRPs [paraprofessionals]," said social worker Susan Hickey.

Some days, the union brought additional members in for a particular topic. For instance, Mayle invited special education teachers to "tell the board what your day is like. Tell them why we need to enforce state law.

"I had members breaking down in tears," Mayle said. "And the board had to sit there and take it."

It felt good to make management feel guilty. But more than that, it was a wake-up call for the board to see how smart and articulate the rank and filers were—showcasing how prepared the union was for the upcoming fight, and what a formidable adversary the members would be. "Our people know way more about the schools than they do, and we proved it to them day after day," Mayle said.

Practice Vote

Senate Bill 7, which had passed the Illinois legislature in 2011, required CTU to get yes votes from 75 percent of all members (not just of those voting) before calling a strike. That is, it would take nearly 20,000 people voting yes to sanction a walkout.

This was supposed to be impossible. "In effect they wouldn't have the ability to strike," gloated Jonah Edelman of the corporate education reform group Stand for Children, which pushed for this rule. Edelman's group had researched past contract votes and found 48 percent was the greatest share of the membership CTU had been able to muster. (For more on SB7, see Chapter 7.)

CTU leaders were convinced 75 percent wasn't impossible—but no one could deny it was a tall order. They knew they needed

Labor Notes Conference

The weekend before the May 10 citywide practice vote, CTU sent 150 members to the biennial national conference of Labor Notes, held May 4-6 in Chicago. The conference brought together 1,500 union leaders and rank-and-file activists from across the country and around the world.

Some were reformers like CORE who had won leadership in their locals; many had led strikes themselves, such as the Wisconsin teachers or an Egyptian unionist who talked about a decade-long strike wave there. And many fellow Chicago unionists were there, too—Transit Union members were particularly prominent in their orange "Occupy Transit" T-shirts.

Jim West, jimwestphoto.com

When high school teacher Jen Johnson spoke about the stakes in CTU's looming strike, the assembled national and international crowd roared.

"Our members saw that people were looking to Chicago," Norine Gutekanst said. "It reinforced the gravity of what we were doing—the importance of it. I think it also opened up their eyes to this really wonderful wealth of organizing and connectivity... It helped us to see that we were part of something much bigger." ✿

to vote before the school year was over, while the issues were hot and members were having daily conversations with each other—and they couldn't go into the vote cold.

In early spring 2012 a delegate decided to conduct a straw poll at one school on whether to strike: "a stroke of brilliance," said Pope. When the delegate announced the school's result—a unanimous yes—to the House of Delegates, the response was "electrifying."

Other schools soon followed suit with their own mock strike votes. The activity was popular with the members, by now incensed at the school board. The union office would get calls from delegates: "My staff met yesterday and we voted 98 percent to strike." And when organizers went out to schools for meetings, they would ask for a show of hands: "How many here would vote for a strike?" By April, 150 schools had voted overwhelmingly to strike in these informal polls, CTU leaders told the press.

But the union needed a comprehensive snapshot of its strength, in all schools at once. So the Contract Action Committees took a formal, district-wide, one-day dry run on May 10.

This practice vote worked on multiple levels. It was a way to get committee members out talking to people about the issues, and a signal to members that a strike vote was coming. But most crucially, it was a way to test the rank-and-file organizers' capacity to mobilize supporters. They would have to drive turnout on a scale they had not experienced before.

Leaders planned the practice vote to closely mimic how the actual strike vote would work. Delegates in each building received paper ballots and instructions by mail. They ran the vote, tallied the ballots, and phoned in the results. Organizers compiled the numbers on giant wall charts in the union's central war room.

The ballots had a four-question poll with questions designed to elicit a yes ("Do the Board's bargaining proposals disrespect CTU members?")—without actually invoking the word "strike." That way the union could use the vote results in public communications that emphasized the issues teachers were mad about, not the prospect of a strike still months away.

The answers to the survey questions would, of course, be overwhelmingly yeses. The important number to tally in each school would be how many ballots the union could collect.

In some schools—for instance, those without delegates, those with bully principals, and those where most teachers were relatively new—leaders thought support might still be weak. The schools with fewer ballots returned would reveal the areas where organizers needed to focus most.

The numbers came back strong: Ninety-eight percent rejected the board's proposals, with more than 80 percent of members participating—a clear sign that the contract campaign had worked. Many ballots bore handwritten comments like "We must go on strike!" or "I'm ready to strike!"

Rally

Three weeks before the last day of school, 7,000 members in red CTU T-shirts swarmed downtown May 23 to an after-school

rally and march. Many came on 100 union-sponsored buses; others carpooled.

"It was beautiful, because some people were still afraid, even though they showed up there," said Vinson. "When we actually got there, when we were in the theater, the atmosphere was so uplifting. Everybody was in red. We knew at this time we were going to have to do something."

For the first time, "we set an example that it's not just two or three at each school—it was all of the staff," Sanders said. From her group of 40 citywide paraprofessionals, about 35 attended. She hadn't let people get away with excuses to miss it: when they said, "I have to pick up my children," she replied, "Pick up your children and meet me here."

The signs said "Yes to Respect," "Yes to Smaller Classes," and "Yes to Student Needs." The huge turnout bolstered the rising mood of exhilaration and power. Teachers sang along to Dolly Parton's "9 to 5" and Aretha Franklin's "Respect." Two parents and a high school student gave stirring speeches.

"There was a different kind of excitement about standing up," remembered Adam Heenan, a teacher at Curie Metro High. Sure, teachers were excited to be making headlines, but it was more than that. "New teachers, young teachers that had never been part of this movement before, could see themselves as part of it without feeling guilty," he said. "This is not about teachers being greedy; this is about teaching and learning conditions.

"Young teachers who have no history of unionism in their families, even in their cities, they won't come out to stuff—but that rally was the turning point. I was so proud that teachers from my school wanted to go."

During a pause in Karen Lewis's speech, someone screamed "Strike!" and the whole Auditorium Theatre took up the chant. "Strike! Strike! Strike!" echoed through the hall—led by members on the floor, not officers.

Some leaders had been wary of Communications Director Stephanie Gadlin's idea to invite press to the rally and make it spectacular: they feared revealing their plans. "But she was right," Gutekanst said. "It was this exhilarating, pulsating event." The great turnout showed how far teachers had come—and the thrill of the action propelled them forward.

"It was exactly what was needed to make sure when the time came to get a strike vote, we were ready," Vinson said.

After rallying, the red-shirted teachers took over the streets of Chicago. A wave of CTU members merged with the union-sponsored group Stand Up Chicago to march 10,000 strong on Chicago's Mercantile Exchange. Together they protested the $77

Sarah Jane Rhee, loveandstrugglephotos.com

The May 23 CTU rally filled Auditorium Theater with a sea of red shirts.

million-a-year subsidy the derivatives marketplace received from the state and called for a small tax on all financial transactions made in Illinois through the Exchange, to pay for good local jobs.

Thousands of Stand Up protesters and the downtown public greeted CTU members with cheers and support—helping calm the fears of those who had been worried about the public's reaction if they were to strike.

"It made me proud to be a teacher, a union teacher," said Parker.

The various assessments—the T-shirt days, the open letter, the mock strike vote, the rallies—were all "tests we created for ourselves," as Potter put it. And CTU was passing its own tests with flying colors. The union was ready for the contract campaign's climactic hurdle.

Strike Vote

After the mock vote and the rally, CTU organizers now knew they had both the support and the organization to do the seemingly impossible. Still, casting a real vote for a strike would be a bolder step than any they'd asked members to take yet—and 20,000 people had to take this courageous leap at once, no easy feat of coordination.

The politicians who had passed SB7 had probably assumed the vote would take place on a single day—but that wasn't specified in the law, union leaders realized. Since some people are sick or out of town on any given day, they decided to hold voting open for three days, June 6-8. Members left no stone unturned: a delegation from Beard School even made a trip to a rehab hospital to bring a ballot to a co-worker recovering from surgery.

The board had also assumed that the union would hold the vote much later. But leaders realized it would have been nearly impossible to hold the vote in the summer; it needed to be held in the buildings, before members left for vacation. "Just like the three days of voting," said Mayle, "this was another way we outfoxed the law."

Just as in the practice round, a delegate ran the voting at each school, but this time the union collected all the physical ballots and counted them in one central location. To guard against accusations of fraud, a worker center ally, Arise Chicago, recruited clergy to observe the count, which took place each of the three nights.

The district supervisors worked long days. Each morning they were in early, talking to people before school, reminding them to vote. Then after work they hurried downtown to hand-count votes from 4 p.m. to midnight. Clergy members signed their names over the tape when the boxes were sealed for the night, and opened them up again the next day.

Sarah Jane Rhee, loveandstrugglephotos.com

Teachers hoisted effigies of wealthy school board members and the schools CEO at their May 23, 2012, rally.

The "yes" stack of votes was quickly enormous, and the "no" stack tiny—no surprise. But the key was turnout. Near the counting, in a smaller room with walls covered in flip charts, organizers tracked how many votes had come in from each building each day. The next morning, dozens of volunteers (including 30 staffers and members on loan from SEIU Healthcare Illinois/Indiana) would be dispatched to the lower-turnout schools to hand flyers to members on their way in to school, reminding them how important it was that they vote that day—"we need everyone to vote," was the message, "no matter how you're voting."

It took a fourth day to finish counting the more than 24,000 votes. But the results spoke for themselves: 90 percent of teachers—and 98 percent of those voting—had voted to authorize a strike.

As the old saying goes, sometimes the boss is the best organizer. The 75 percent threshold was an anti-union measure, but it also turned out to be a great motivator, adding urgency to the push for every member to vote and for every school to organize a contract action team—things that would be important anyway for a successful strike. "The union had to be at the height of its game," said labor educator Steven Ashby.

Now momentum was on the union's side. Over the summer, CTU brought in several dozen members to work as intern organizers, making sure their colleagues stayed connected to the union and up-to-date on bargaining through the summer break, and doing community outreach too. The interns walked around in their red union T-shirts talking to "parents on the corners, in grocery stores, and walking down the street," said Sanders, one of the participants.

"We told them it wasn't just about more money," she said. "We talked to parents, reassured them, 'Sure, we would like a raise, just like you in your job would like a raise—but the key is conditions in our schools.'"

She would tell them the numbers: Counselors trying to serve 3,000 students each. Case workers at a different school every day of the week. Two or three paraprofessionals in a school that had had five or six a decade earlier. "I always told them, 'When you went to school you were offered music, art; some schools had choirs,'" she said. "'Now they don't offer that. Teachers are overwhelmed with too many students; some have special needs. It's hard when you have 36, 38 kids.'

"We want kids to have the same great education as Rahm Emanuel's children," was Sanders's rap.

The interns also organized community meetings, inviting parents they had met and CTU members who lived in the area. The invited aldermen didn't show up, but local residents came out in force. In her own neighborhood of Englewood, Sanders expected maybe 20 or 30 people to attend—but 100 did. "In the neediest communities you're suffering twice as much," she said. "It was going to be an hour, but it turned out to be two and a half hours."

Arbitrator Offers Raise

SB7—the same law that sought to prevent a strike—also mandated that an arbitrator had to make a fact-finding report and recommendation, and at least one side had to reject it, before CTU could resort to a strike. This report came in July.

The arbitrator, Edward Benn, made economic proposals far more favorable than the city's. He proposed a 15 percent raise (compared to the mayor's 2 percent), nearly enough to match the 20 percent increase in the school day and year that the board wanted to implement. He called for preserving pay increases for years of service and advanced degrees.

But CTU leaders advised delegates to reject the report. It wasn't about the money. "It doesn't address the education issues that we're concerned about," said Mayle. "Things like getting extra art teachers, reducing paperwork for teachers... the things that affect the day-to-day lives of teachers, he really didn't touch on." Of course, the report actually could not address those items, only ruling on mandatory (and therefore strikable) bargaining subjects.

Jim Cavallero, a high school special education teacher and delegate, was surprised at the good parts of the arbitrator's recommendations, given how anti-union Chicago politics had become. But the quality-of-education issues—like smaller classes, computers in the classroom, and nursing and social work services for students—mattered far more than the money, Cavallero said. He hoped CTU would use the arbitrator's salary proposals as a bargaining chip for better programs for students and better working conditions for teachers.

Another reason to reject the report, Mayle said, was that accepting a third-party proposal would send the wrong message for future bargaining. "We don't want to set a precedent where some outsider sets the terms of our contract," she said. "We want to be able to negotiate our contracts."

The union's House of Delegates voted the report down unanimously. The school board also quickly rejected the report's findings, in a closed session. Emanuel slammed the report as "not connected to reality," and the district CEO said raises for teachers would necessitate layoffs and cutbacks.

"The irony is the board kept saying, 'Wait for the fact-finder,'" Mayle observed at the time. "Now that fact-finder said something they don't like."

Scheduled bargaining sessions would continue as planned. But since both the board and the union had rejected the report, CTU was now free to strike after 30 days.

The union won a major victory a few days later, when the city—recognizing the momentum and CTU's power—reached an interim agreement on the longer school day. (For more on the content of the deal, see Chapter 7.) Mayle said the agreement proved that people power and direct action could get the goods. "It only took 10,000 people in the street, a strike authorization vote, and a fact-finder to tell them that they're crazy—but, hey, whatever works!"

Community Allies Lace Up Their Boots

Actions like the May 23 rally had primed community allies for the mass strike mobilizations that were coming. By now they'd struggled in the streets with teachers many times and were practiced at turnout for large events.

Groups on the Community Board held educational events for their members in the lead-up to the strike, breaking down the complexities of contract negotiations and preparing parents for what was in store. Some, like Kenwood Oakland Community Organization, Action Now, and Albany Park Neighborhood Council, canvassed their neighborhoods to drum up support for the impending walkout.

The Community Board groups were also campaigning that summer to get the issue of an elected school board onto the November ballot (see Chapter 6), a demand that dovetailed perfectly with both groups' shared vision of high-quality public schools for all students, regardless of race or income.

Throughout the contract campaign, teachers had also been reaching out to parents one on one. These conversations were focused on "issues like over-testing, crowding of classrooms, the teacher-to-student ratio: things that parents would be concerned with," Bowsky said. Unlike the district, "we weren't bribing parents with iPads or new soccer fields; we were telling parents their children were people that deserved people. We talked to parents about where the rubber hits the road: what we do with the children."

Teachers began by "just trying to engage parents where they were," Cavallero said. Many parents said, "Well, I don't know much about it, but you do a great job with our kids." That was a good place to start. By the time of the strike, said Cavallero, his school had plenty of support from both parents and students.

Strike Notice

Meanwhile, the union and the board were far from a deal. Salaries and health care costs were unresolved, as were disputes over evaluations and discipline. And while the 512 new teachers to be hired under the longer school day agreement would increase the variety of classes offered, the increase amounted to only one additional teacher per school. The change would do nothing to fix the problem of overcrowded classes.

The new longer school day went into effect for some CTU members in mid-August, when 240 schools on a special "Track E" schedule started up. The rest of the district's 600 schools would open their doors to students on September 4. Schools CEO Jean-Claude Brizard soon reported that the longer day was working.

CTU said otherwise. Teachers were being forced to take on other duties during their prep periods, in violation of the agreement. (Teacher unions across the country are perennially forced to fight to defend their prep periods—precious time during the school day spent on devising lesson plans, grading homework, perhaps even calling or meeting with parents. Teachers still work many unpaid hours after school completing these tasks, of course.) Schedules for those in new positions were in constant flux. Assistants and paraprofessionals reported supervising up to 96 kids each during newly implemented recesses.

On August 22, the union's House of Delegates met. Rank-and-file members, though they cannot vote, have the right to attend these meetings, too. About a thousand people came out to this one. CTU leaders explained where both sides' proposals stood, and asked delegates what they wanted to do.

Delegates were outraged at the board's contract proposals, CORE co-chair Al Ramirez reported. "For a person who's paying attention, to see that they want to remove so much of the contract, to gut it," he said, "how they want to impose a new evaluation system, the disrespectful proposal for compensation—and finally that last paragraph on management rights was the last straw. There was a collective groan in the house. There was a chant of 'Hell no, hell no!'"

A motion came from the floor to authorize Lewis to give the board a 10-day strike notice (required under Illinois law) at her discretion, and delegates voted yes.

"It is not a better school day yet," Lewis said at a press conference that day, "and if we just leave it up to these guys, it will never be a better school day."

"It had to be done," said Bowsky. "To me, it's felt like that for a year."

A week later, August 29, Lewis filed the notice. The next day CTU announced its strike date: September 10.

The delegates' vote proved they were ready—but Contract Action Committee members continued their outreach to make sure the rank and file were ready, too. "It was so important to get people to know that it was not something to be afraid of," Heenan said later. "If there were people who'd been on a picket line before, they got a chance to let us know what it was like... We even had someone who'd crossed the picket line 25 years ago talk about why she regretted it."

Practice, Practice, Practice

As the strike date neared, the union held informational pickets to educate parents and to give members a sense of what a picket line might feel like. Members not yet back to work were assigned to go to the early-start schools. Carrying signs proclaiming they were "fighting for the schools Chicago's students deserve," they spoke to parents and passersby about the issues at stake.

About half the early-start schools hosted pickets—and the response from the community was encouraging. At Ruggles Elementary, officers in a police truck honked their horn and blew their whistles to show solidarity. Drivers on their way past Azuela Elementary reached out of their cars to grab solidarity stickers

How Drummond Teachers Got Their Voice Back

One of the schools that hosted an informational picket was Drummond Elementary, a Montessori school in a gentrified neighborhood on the North Side. Drummond was a small school with engaged parents, so on one level teachers knew them well—"but we never talked about meaty stuff," said delegate Anne Carlson, such as "what it was like to be in front of a class and tell them they have to go take a test for two hours. We had the foundation of being close, but just never crossing that one line."

The picket got things rolling. One of the parents helped to flyer during the picket. Another helped organize an informational meeting in the neighborhood, held August 28 at a bar one of the parents owned. Two teachers and a dozen parents showed up. Someone watched the kids in the back.

The relaxed atmosphere away from Drummond helped lower people's anxieties. "When you're meeting in school you feel the walls have ears," Carlson said, because of "that culture of fear that has been created in public schools." At last, parents and teachers could talk more openly about their educational concerns.

"It was very eye-opening for parents," Carlson said. "This was the first time teachers were able to open up about things we had been experiencing for years... We could breathe a sigh of relief that we all care."

Things took off after that. "We told the parents, 'We would love if you took this on and ran with it,'" Carlson said. And they did: the parents posted info on the Parent Teacher Organization Facebook page, put together a flyer explaining the issues and telling ways parents could support the strikers, cross-checked it with teachers, and passed it out at a schoolwide picnic.

The Drummond meeting not only laid the groundwork for strong strike support. It also planted the seed of a parent-teacher group that would go on to fight over-testing after the strike. ✿

Sarah Jane Rhee, loveandstrugglephotos.com

from teachers holding signs on the street corner.

Protesters at Arnold Mireles Academy were warmly received when they decided to march down the neighborhood's main strip chanting, "We need teachers, we need books, we need the money that Rahm took!"

"People were coming out of stores to take literature. People were putting up fists and waving and continuing to honk as they went down the street," reported Bowsky. "Then we went through the neighborhood and chanted and talked with people we met." She had been a leader in efforts at Seward Academy, but was pleased that some of her colleagues stepped up to lead the turnout for their assigned picket. "They're taking it upon themselves to do something, and called me and invited me," she said—"even though I was already going."

Veronica McDaniel, a middle school librarian, was glad for the chance to connect with community members and dispel media rumors. She asked parents she met on the picket line to "tell me what your kids have in their schools. We're trying to get decent programs in all our schools."

"It is hard to overstate the transformational effect it had on members as they directly talked to parents about the union's struggle and succeeded in winning support," Luskin said.

During the 10-day waiting period between the strike notice and the strike, members also went out to community organizations, churches, and train stops to speak about what was coming up and ask for support. Again the response was overwhelmingly positive.

"You talk to people on the street, sometimes they don't have kids in school," Vinson said, "but it got back to, in lots of the neighborhoods, not only attacks on schools but attacks on housing. We talked about fair wages. We found ways to connect to all these issues. If parents are trying to take care of a family on minimum wage, those stresses show up in the classroom. You can't fault parents for their level of engagement when they're dealing with so much stress."

Bowsky and another teacher visited mass at Holy Cross Parish, at the invitation of Father Bruce Wellems, to explain the strike issues to a couple hundred community members. "That particular priest was heavily involved in the neighborhood," Bowsky said, "so he was able to relate it to what else was going on, including the possible closure of hospitals that serve the whole community, and explain it in Spanish to the people."

The last week in August, the remaining teachers started back with a full week of scheduled professional development days before students would return. "That was like a gift," Heenan said—providing plenty of opportunities to talk with co-workers about strike preparations. "I laid out logistics, talked over strike bulletins. We went over all the details, from where strike headquarters would be to what the Twitter handle would be."

The day before students would return to school—and a week before the strike deadline—CTU joined dozens of other unions for a Labor Day rally. The Chicago Federation of Labor had not sponsored a Labor Day rally for years. But this year the Democratic National Convention would overlap with Labor Day. CTU leaders knew many prominent Chicago and national labor leaders would be in attendance, rubbing shoulders with Rahm Emanuel and other Democratic officials who were leading the attack on CTU. They worried that the mayor and the press would paint a picture of a lack of official union support for the impending strike.

So CTU hatched a plan for Labor Day. Activists reached out to key unions and community organizations. Once these groups were signed on, and the character of the rally as pro-CTU, pro-strike, anti-Rahm, and anti-corporate was assured, they took the event to the Federation for endorsement.

The City Gears Up

The city, too, was clearly taking the strike threat seriously. "Mayor 1%" Emanuel started to take a more active role. His education advisor and the CPS board president were among those who joined negotiations to attempt to avert a strike. The district asked principals to report any union activity they found disruptive as "harassment/threat-type activity."

While dozens of teachers and allies rallied outside an August 22 board of education meeting, next to a giant inflatable rat on loan from the Teamsters, the board voted to spend $25 million on alternate arrangements for students in the event of a strike. The money would hire organizations like local YMCAs to provide food, shelter, and "non-instructional services."

Teachers who'd seen their schools denied resources for years were outraged that the district could find the money for its strike plan so easily. "That's a lot of money," fumed Ramirez. "Tell me it couldn't be used for something else a lot better."

Lessons

⇨ CTU's contract campaign relied on tried-and-true organizing fundamentals, including a member-to-member action network and detailed numerical tracking of the union's level of support at each school.

⇨ An inclusive process to develop bargaining demands, involving many meetings with different subsets of the membership, ensured everyone had a stake in the campaign.

⇨ Actions that members organized at a local level, which had rank and filers initiating their own plans and using their own voices, were crucial in building members' skills and confidence while expanding the entire union's capacity.

⇨ A series of escalating actions—from wearing red to a practice vote—built members' confidence and repeatedly tested their support before the real strike vote.

⇨ CTU didn't let the law and the legislature's stumbling blocks back the union into a corner. Leaders took what management had designed as an impossibly high hurdle—the 75 percent strike vote requirement—and used it as a challenge to organize an almost unanimous strike vote.

⇨ Union leaders didn't promise that a strike would win, just that it was the only chance to strike a blow for the students and for a decent contract.

⇨ During negotiations, members of the bargaining team took controversial questions back to their schools to find out what co-workers thought.

⇨ Overwhelmingly, parents responded warmly to being educated about the contract fight, when the outreach came from a teacher they trusted.

⇨ A mass rally was an emotional turning point, emboldening teachers by demonstrating their power and the broad public support they had won.

9

Strike

School Board President David Vitale shook visibly, late on the evening of Sunday, September 9, as he announced that talks had broken down. He emphasized the concessions the board had made on union members' economic issues, saying, "This should satisfy most of their needs." He claimed the board was unsure what more teachers wanted.

Not a half-hour later, with throngs of red-shirted union members flanking the doors, CTU officers emerged stoically from the union office to announce the strike.

The two sides were still far apart on teacher evaluations and recall rights. More important, said Vice President Jesse Sharkey, were "pedagogical issues" like small class sizes; a curriculum of language, art, music, and physical education for all students; and nursing and social work services inside schools to address the many needs poor students bring to the schoolhouse door that hurt their academic performance.

At its core, the strike would be nothing less than a face-off between two conflicting visions of public education.

"People were already so fed up that, even though a strike was scary, they weren't horrified by the idea," said Jen Johnson, a member of the team coordinating strike logistics. "We were organizationally, mentally, and emotionally prepared."

At last, long-laid plans began to grind into motion. That night, bargaining team member Jim Cavallero sent the word by text message to the four strike captains at his small school, Chicago Academy High. Each had 10 members to call. "We'd already talked about what we were going to do if we went out, and each person had a role," Cavallero said. "One made sure there was going to be coffee; one made sure we knew where people were going to park."

On the Picket Lines

Monday morning, September 10, a constant chorus of horns blared in support as members and students alike joined steadily growing picket lines in front of each of the city's 600 schools, plus board headquarters. Teenagers stood with their teachers and cheered, waving signs and wielding noisemakers. "I saw parents, too, at every school I visited," said Financial Secretary Kristine Mayle. "At some, parents brought grills and cooked breakfast for teachers at the picket line."

The Contract Action Committee members turned into strike captains, each responsible for a team of 10 members on the line and checking in with them on plans and morale. Each school had one head captain (often the delegate), who stayed in touch with a strike coordinator for a cluster of schools. The district supervisors took on the job of strike coordinator.

Strike Trainings

Union staff gave a series of strike trainings in the late summer, open to Contract Action Committee members and anyone else each school wanted to send. According to Staff Coordinator Jackson Potter, the trainings covered:

Timeline of a strike day—picket at schools in the morning, go to shared location in the afternoon, local activities organized by your school in between if possible.

Rationale—why the union was striking; the latest updates from bargaining.

Legal rights—your right to be on the sidewalk, a phone number to reach a lawyer if you are told you have to leave.

Logistics—how to deal with bathrooms and parking.

Phone trees—what to say to members to get them to join the picket.

Picket line etiquette—don't get into heated debates with hostile people; don't antagonize parents who bring their kids to the holding centers.

Chants—every location should have a chant leader.

Daily bulletin—strike coordinators distributed these to the lines.

Besides the nuts and bolts, the trainings also covered how to reach out to parents and in school neighborhoods, how best to talk about strike issues with parents, and organizing visible local actions. ✿

The heart of the strike captain's work each day was to make sure every teacher was there at the picket line, with signs. If someone didn't show up, the captain would call or get someone else in the phone tree to call—"Are you sick? Do you need a ride? Are you at a different picket line today?"

At Curie Metro High, a big school with 260 teachers and 22 strike captains, "we could not have gotten through this without using a program called GroupMe," Adam Heenan said. The free app allows members on a cell phone list to send out mass text messages to the whole group.

Then the head captains would get on the phone with their strike coordinators, reporting what was good and what was bad that day; what great new picket line tactics members had come up with; who wasn't there and how they were following up; any problems with cops or scabs.

The strike coordinators would make rounds, visiting each school in their cluster of eight to 12 at least once a day—bringing materials from headquarters (picket signs and a daily one-page newsletter called "On the Line"), bargaining updates, and plans for the afternoon's rallies.

Strike coordinators also had the authority to reassign pickets in their area to support weaker schools or those who needed a morale boost. They coordinated between schools to move members

On the Line, CTU's daily strike bulletin.

when there were opportunities for high visibility, and occasionally quickly mobilized members for local actions, such as when the union got wind that the mayor would be at an event nearby.

Paraprofessional Charlotte Sanders visited eight or nine schools each day. She showed up at the first one at 5:30 a.m. to buoy morale as needed. "If one school needed more assistance, I would spend more quality time with those members," she said. She also kept an eye out for problems such as administrators trying to kick strikers off the grounds.

Overall, "I was shocked at how many people came out," Sanders said. "You think people are going to think, 'I've got a day off,' but at 6 a.m. they were on the line… One teacher had a two-month-old baby. Her husband sat in the car with the baby, and she walked the line."

And it wasn't just CTU members. "Parents came every day bringing us coffee," said Anne Carlson of Drummond Elementary. "We never had to buy food. Parents showed up every day at 6:30; students would come too. They created their own signs and would march around the school."

Not all parents got involved, of course—but "those that were involved came out every single morning," reported Andrea Parker, a teacher at Curtis Elementary. "One parent of a third-grader in particular—sometimes before the teachers were there, she was there."

Spirits were high. Some people picketed with signs, others sat in lawn chairs, chatting. There was plenty of chanting, dancing, and food, recalled *Labor Notes* reporter Theresa Moran, who visited a number of sites. Many picket lines "incorporated the neighborhood flavor," she said.

Some people brought homemade drums. At Kenwood High, someone set up speakers in the back of a truck to blast music, and

Red Badge of Courage

"Your uniform every day was your union shirt—or to wear something red," Charlotte Sanders said. She had told co-workers before the strike, "This is going to be your red badge of courage. You will be able to signify with other people who you are." And it was true: community members came to recognize the shirts and what they stood for. "Even after the strike, people would see our shirts and say, 'You're with the union! I'm for you,'" she said. ✿

Lauren McCadney Photography

teachers line-danced; an impromptu march took the music truck past Obama's house and the house of the school board president. On the West Side, teachers and parents at a couple of elementary schools got together for a barbecue at a playground, with a band playing live music. A radio station personality came around dropping off doughnuts to different picket locations.

People joked that "we were having too much fun on strike," said Tammie Vinson, the delegate at Emmet Elementary. Her picket line had 100 percent participation. "It brought people together as a stronger unit. We had a regular social conversation we weren't able to have during the school day," she said. "We'd go to breakfast or lunch together after picketing. We became closer as a staff. When the strike was over we still kept in contact."

When strikers marched through the neighborhood near Seward Academy, the general response from drivers and passersby was "fantastic"—but "we did get a few thumbs down," said teacher Kimberly Bowsky. At one point she got into a yelling match with people on a nearby stoop. They seemed mad about their own bad experiences with school; she tried to make them see how the problem wasn't individual teachers but a system that set teachers up to fail. Two were convinced, and even started holding union signs to show their support. "Every day for the rest of the week those people sat out on their stoop and supported us," she recalled.

"That's the great thing about what we're doing," Bowsky said: "it's issue-based. You could hate teachers or be fearful of teachers. But once the community and the parents and the students saw there were issues here, you could put down whatever and work on the issues."

One day, Curtis Elementary and four other schools marched to an alderman's office and picketed outside, demanding he tell the mayor he supported the teachers, Parker recalled. Another day, several schools got together to go picket by the expressway where they'd be visible to passing cars. "We had a lot of unity," she said, "not just with teachers in our school but with people from other schools in our area."

"We had serious parties on our line," Heenan said. "Our show choir came out every day. Kids in a Jeep would drive up and down the street honking."

Overall, CTU estimated about 95 percent of members participated in school pickets. And almost none crossed: about 15 scabs altogether, out of 27,000 members. That's 99.9 percent strike participation—a sign how effective CTU's intense contract campaign had been. (The few scabs later faced internal charges and were kicked out of the union.)

Picketing the Holding Centers

The district didn't try to keep all the schools open. It designated 144 schools as "holding centers" where students could go for food and supervision between 8:30 a.m. and 12:30 p.m. Police stood by the entrances to watch the few who came.

This cost $25 million, and the union questioned whether it was money well spent. The facilities were run by staff from the district's central office and clergy—people with no background in education or childcare. A manual for those working the holding centers instructed them to play games like "Simon says" and to "communicate with words."

Ironically, the manuals drew attention to the same poor building conditions teachers were raising concerns about. District employees were warned to dress for classrooms with no air conditioners and not to count on having a refrigerator or microwave available. CTU spokeswoman Stephanie Gadlin called the plan "the equivalent of opening a fire station without firefighters and giving a bunch of lawyers, accountants, and clerical workers a few fire hoses and rubber boots."

Tim Meegan was one of 10 strike captains at one holding

John A. Harris, Jr.

center, Roosevelt High. He was impressed with CTU's hands-off, decentralized approach to running the strike—and how efficiently this worked. "I basically got marching orders from the union and decided how to implement that at Roosevelt," he said.

Meegan would arrive at 6 a.m. to take photos of every car that entered the parking lot and make sure someone was always on the lookout for scabs. (Picket captains were not supposed to get into confrontation with scabs, just note and report them.) Roosevelt takes up an entire city block, so covering all the parking lot entrances was no small task, and a busy transit stop a block away had to be covered, too.

The 10 strike captains, each leading a team of 8 to 10 union members, rotated in two-hour shifts through the different assignments: the main picket line, farther-out posts, and canvassing the neighborhood.

The holding centers didn't attract many students—or "hold" them for long. "Only a dozen kids showed up," Meegan said. "They left after an hour or so because they were bored, and they came out and joined the picket line with us."

Mid-week, union leaders tried switching it up, shifting from 600 separate picket lines to consolidated picketing at just the 144 holding centers. Members whose schools didn't offer much opportunity for contact with the public preferred this, but for many, this idea wasn't as popular. "People really liked being at their own schools," Organizing Director Norine Gutekanst said. "They enjoyed bonding with each other."

Explosion of Community Enthusiasm

It wasn't just teachers who showed up in force September 10; community groups did, too. "There was such an explosion of activity," said Alex Han, a Service Employees (SEIU) and Stand Up Chicago organizer who was loaned to work with the Community Board (see Chapter 6) during the strike. "Albany Park Neighborhood Council would just call me and say, 'Our parents are marching from school to school every day to join every picket line.'"

"Teachers are part of our community even if they don't live here," explained Raul Botello of the Albany Park organization, which brought 200 people to CTU's big downtown rally the first day. "We had a mini-movement in our own community. We turned out about 1,000 people to five actions. We literally would have solidarity marches supporting our teachers every other day."

One day the organization joined with strikers to march on Alderman Dick Mell—to let him know they weren't about to let Roosevelt High be turned over to a charter company. Another day it held a standing-room-only forum for parents, students, and teachers.

In the lead-up to the strike Botello's group and others pulled members together to canvass their neighbors. During the strike, they joined the pickets, flyered their neighborhoods, went with teachers to aldermen's offices, held community forums, organized day camps for out-of-school children, coordinated buses to bring people to the daily rallies, and organized their own pro-teacher rallies and press events independently of the union.

Logan Square Neighborhood Association, like many other formal and informal groups across the city, organized a "freedom camp" to provide childcare to out-of-school kids. A week of lessons on movements led by Cesar Chavez and Martin Luther King, Jr. capped off with parents and students demonstrating in support of the strikers. Waving handmade signs, the kids performed the civil rights classic "We Shall Not Be Moved" for beaming teachers.

"It was a very intense 10 days," said Community Board member Rico Gutstein. "I think community members doing strike support were as engaged and active in mobilizing people as many teachers."

The Community Board served as a clearinghouse, coordinating actions. The group met three times during the strike and its members corresponded daily over phone and email to discuss updates and what each organization had planned. "Most of it was coordinating natural activity that community groups were doing," Han said.

The community groups were important in keeping the strike's themes front and center. Union leaders had to tread a careful legal line in what they said publicly, since the union could not legally walk out over key issues such as class size and curriculum. Neighborhood activists could be blunter.

When the Kenwood Oakland Community Organization (KOCO) sent students and parents to speak at strike rallies, "we began to carry the message, because we knew there were some things that the union could not bring to the forefront," said organizer Jitu Brown. "We pushed the concept that a broken school system was the reason our teachers were striking. It was not over money but rampant closing of schools, firing teachers en masse, which destabilizes student education."

Voices of Youth in Chicago Education (VOYCE), a city-wide high school organizing project, held a September 12 protest against high-stakes testing, highlighting how standardized tests misrepresent and punish students and teachers alike. More than 150 students and parents rallied with teachers on the Wells High picket line to speak out against the barrage of standardized tests they were forced to undergo. Holding a dizzyingly long garland of 12,000 pencils—each representing an hour spent in standardized testing over the course of a year—students chanted "1-2-3-4, more than just a testing score!"

Even though money poured in from corporate education reform groups, who ran nonstop TV ads against the teachers—and even though the city and the school district together had 30 communications staffers, while CTU had three—the public sided with the union. As President Karen Lewis put it, "They tied our hands and we still kicked their asses."

The profound, widespread support didn't spring up overnight, of course. Years of work had led up to this moment: CORE's and CTU's close-knit organizing with parent and community activists, fighting school closures and developing the Community Board. (Read about that in Chapters 3, 4, 6, and 7.)

Talking Honestly with Parents

Members were encouraged to canvass neighborhoods on foot to reach parents who weren't involved, as a regular part of picket duty. When it was your team's turn, you'd take some leaflets, break into pairs, and walk in four directions away from the school, taking a list of addresses and parent information. A handful of supportive parents canvassed alongside teachers. Activists had been trained in listening to parents' concerns and drawing out the links between what they heard and the strike.

These conversations were a chance to counter the city's anti-teacher propaganda. The union's proposed wage increase (comparable to the longer school day and year that the mayor had declared) was a big target in the press. Teachers could legally strike only over wages and benefits—so that was their bargaining chip—but they had to make sure parents understood the strike was about much more.

Even though technically "we couldn't strike for smaller class sizes, for a shorter school day, actually even for having art, music, gym," these were the real themes of the strike, Vinson said. The district had also killed vocational programs that neighborhood schools had once been able to offer, such as shop and drafting.

Parker said when she told people about the threatened school closures, some would get angry: "This is not fair, this is politically motivated. Why are they doing this to you all?" they would exclaim. "We told them we were fighting to make sure kids get books on the first day, to make art and music for every student," she said. "When I was growing up, we had all those things. Now they don't have art or music or even a library teacher."

Before the strike, teachers were often afraid to be too critical

Sarah Jane Rhee, loveandstrugglephotos.com

Sarah Jane Rhee, loveandstrugglephotos.com

of the problems with their schools—even when talking with parents. What if being too honest got you fired? Members didn't want to make their school look bad, but desperately wanted to tell the public about the real causes of their school's problems.

"We're stuck in this system where we feel trapped and not able to talk to parents," Carlson said. "We might be disciplined or evaluated... Parents made assumptions about teachers and vice versa. Both thought the other wouldn't understand. When we started talking about things that mattered to parents, we realized we both love these children."

So "during the strike, the gloves were off," said Meegan. "For the first time, teachers were talking directly to community about things we were afraid to say... Once you get over that fear, there's a feeling of freedom and liberation."

That feeling lasted even after the strike was over. "I refuse to go back to being afraid," Meegan said later.

"The parents kept us going," Sanders said. "They made us feel like, 'It's not just a job—you are part of our family.' You could put whatever you want on the news, but parents know what was right and what was wrong... At first the mayor was all bark, but after he got caught up by a few parents he got silent, he never even talked."

Social Justice High School teacher Dave Hernandez said, "The biggest takeaway I've learned so far is the importance of a deliberate connection between parents, teachers, and students."

After the strike, the board terminated two teacher union leaders from Social Justice High, along with the principal. CTU members quickly used the relationships they'd built, jointly organizing community meetings with concerned parents and students. After these led to community canvasses and a student sit-in inside the school, CPS officials relented, reinstating the teachers, the principal, and the academic programs they had just cut.

Noon Debrief

Each day at noon, the 79 strike coordinators plus five regional strike leaders would gather to check in and debrief at the Teamsters Local 705 hall, where the union was basing its operations. CTU's offices, on the fourth floor of a downtown office building, would have been much too small. Luckily, Local 705 offered its majestic building, complete with a beautiful mural celebrating the 1997 strike against UPS. The strikers hung a huge "CTU Strike Headquarters" sign on the front of the building.

It was the perfect spot for a strike hub, providing ample space inside and out for the buzz of ongoing activity: loading picket signs here, producing the bulletin there, wall charts over there, field debrief here. The Chicago Teachers Solidarity Committee—formed by parents and local labor and Occupy activists, with labor educator Steven Ashby among its leaders—beefed up the headquarters staffing. "You can park with your hazards on to pick up signs and materials from 5 a.m. to 3 p.m. on the first day and 6 a.m. to 3 p.m. each day thereafter," the first day's strike bulletin announced. "Please come by the Teamster Auditorium to volunteer, break bread with solidarity folks or get the latest on our strike."

After the strike coordinators got a bite to eat, Gutekanst would start the meeting by asking people to share some of the day's best stories. "Hands would just shoot in the air," remembered Ashby: an impromptu march on the local alderman, a school in a Mexican community where parents had set up tables at the picket line and were cooking for teachers on the spot. "We were all a little bit jealous of that!" Gutekanst said.

During the meeting, strike coordinators would also fill out a daily form, reporting turnout and other specifics from their areas. Union leaders would brief them on any updates from bargaining, highlights of the past 24 hours, and plans for that afternoon's rally

and the next day's picket. They would also hand out the next issue of the one-page strike bulletin, which included helpful phone
numbers (including a food pantry and a credit union for loans;
the union had no strike fund), schedule info, suggested chants,
short bargaining updates, photos from the picket lines, and even
cartoons making light of the situation.

Labor Solidarity

CTU had worked with Occupy Chicago since its launch
the previous fall, so it made perfect sense when activists in the
movement's Labor Working Group launched a Chicago Teachers
Solidarity Committee in June 2012. (See Chapter 7.) About 110
people came to the first meeting, and the group started handing
out flyers in parks and reaching out to community groups and
unions to build support for the anticipated strike.

It was the kind of outreach a local labor council might do,
Ashby said—but the Chicago Federation of Labor wasn't doing it,
because many local labor leaders were not willing to confront the
hard-charging mayor. So the Solidarity Committee picked up the
slack, supplying the headquarters with committed volunteers who
did a variety of nuts-and-bolts tasks.

The unions who got most involved were those already mobilizing in fights of their own. AFSCME distributed solidarity
stickers to librarians citywide who had just had their own nas-
ty contract fight. SEIU Healthcare Illinois/Indiana (HCII) was
headed into contract campaigns for homecare and childcare state
employees while also facing the closing of safety-net hospitals. It
loaned staff to the teachers to help marshal the afternoon actions
and plan march routes. HCII also organized a "telephone town
hall" that 4,469 of its members joined in on, to discuss the strike,
the school board's racism, and the connection to their members as
both parents and unionists.

Other key allies included AFSCME state workers, city bus
drivers, and the Grassroots Collaborative. Donations poured in
from around the country—more than $100,000—with the money
used to cover strike expenses.

By the time the teachers struck, the other unions representing
workers in the schools (the Operating Engineers, UNITE HERE,
and SEIU, whose members included maintenance workers, janitors, cafeteria workers, bus aides, special education assistants, and

security officers) had settled their contracts and kept working. Some early talk of the unions' coordinating their contract campaigns didn't pan out.

Nonetheless, members of the other unions found ways of showing solidarity, like wearing red in the lead-up to and during the strike. A handful of SEIU Local 1 janitors held a one-day sympathy strike, giving up a day's pay to show their solidarity by walking picket lines with CTU.

The relationship among the unions improved in the joint campaign against closures in the 2012-13 school year. (Read more in Chapter 11.) "I think the strike helped," said Mayle. "I think

AFL-CIO

people thought we were crazy at first, maybe a little incompetent, naïve—and once we pulled it off, it changed people's perceptions of us."

The American Federation of Teachers, CTU's parent, offered money, communications staffers, and organizers. Lewis accepted the help as long as it was under the local's direction. AFT staffers worked on strike support, rather than negotiations. Once the strike started, President Randi Weingarten "didn't really have much choice," said Debby Pope, a strike coordinator. At one point Weingarten stopped by to give her support; CTU officers had her introduce herself to the board's bargainers, but then it was time to leave for a rally.

Afternoon Rallies

In the afternoons, teachers and supporters from all across the city would gather for mass marches and rallies. On Monday, 35,000 turned out—a "sea of people," *Substance News* said—to surround CPS's downtown headquarters, red T-shirts packing the streets as far as you could see in either direction. On scores of handmade signs, teachers, students, parents, and community members declared what the strike was about:

"My students need desks!"

"I have 43 kindergarten students ALL DAY"

"My textbooks are from 1986"

"Only 24% of CPS schools have art and music!"

 "Youth demand respect 4 teachers"

"Keep public schools safe from private corporate monsters"

"I teach my students to stand up for themselves. Here's my real-life example"

"Your kids deserve what Rahm's kids get"

"Democratic Party: where are you?"

Tuesday the march started at district headquarters again, then moved on major downtown boulevards to confront corporations receiving TIFs and tax breaks. Wednesday, members split up to rally at three high schools and marched through the neighborhoods. Thursday was a picket led by the Grassroots Collaborative. They targeted billionaire school board member Penny Pritzker, the Hyatt heiress, highlighting the $5 million in TIF money her new hotel had received.

Marching tens of thousands strong was a huge thrill—"this

is the best I have felt in my entire teaching career!" one teacher told a video blogger—and it put the union's support and power on display to everyone, even downtown businesspeople who might not be seeing it in their own tony neighborhoods.

On Friday, instead of rallying, teachers went door to door in their schools' neighborhoods once more. Saturday was another mass rally, drawing busloads of supporters—especially fellow teachers—from around Illinois and even from out of state, including Madison, Milwaukee, Minneapolis, and Dearborn, Michigan.

Delegates Vote to Continue the Strike

While members across the city picketed, the core bargaining team was on its own grueling schedule: negotiating almost nonstop and squeezing in a few hours of sleep when possible. It was up to leaders outside the room—members of the big bargaining team, the executive board, and the strike coordinators and captains—to keep their fingers on members' pulse and meet with the bargainers to communicate how things felt in the field.

The core team neared a tentative agreement late in the week and started making public statements to that effect. But on Saturday evening—after another big day of rallying—the frontline leaders met with the bargainers and argued that members were too fired up for a meeting of delegates alone to call an end to the strike. Members would want time for everyone to read any agreement and make the decision together.

When the officers emerged from a marathon 27-hour session on Sunday with a more-or-less final proposal, they had just time to run home and take a shower before the scheduled House of Delegates meeting. There, they presented the contract offer to the delegates—acknowledging frankly that it was less than what they deserved, but explaining why they thought it an acceptable deal that beat back the worst of the assault. They cautioned members that public support would ebb as the strike went on, and that Mayor Emanuel would likely push for an injunction to stop it.

Sure enough, the delegates wanted to continue the strike. They didn't think it was fair to make such a "momentous decision" without member input, Jen Johnson explained. "It's not just a contract vote," she said. "We're on strike and it's a different context. People felt very strongly about having a little time with their members."

Bittersweet Victory

"There were like six standing ovations," Debby Pope said, during the joyful meeting when delegates finally came back together after two days of rank-and-file deliberation. Delegates overflowed with a feeling of "tremendous sisterhood and brotherhood."

Yet for Pope there was a bittersweet moment, after Kristine Mayle explained a new contract provision that might sound tiny to an outsider. It said that "teachers can do their lesson plans in any format or font as long as they submit them," Pope said.

"That's what got the first standing ovation. Because teachers have been so browbeaten, so de-professionalized—that statement which didn't cost the board a single dollar was so meaningful to people." ☼

The officers quickly agreed. "It was a test of leadership," said Ashby. "Some leaders might say, 'You voted for me, you need to trust me.'" But, after all, CTU's officers had said over and over, "Members run this union." They meant it.

Delegates voted overwhelmingly to continue the strike for two more days and to vote again Tuesday night, after the 27,000 members had had time to read and discuss the contract. In the past members had felt that contracts were rammed down their throats hurriedly. "We had activated people to the point they didn't want to vote until they had read the whole thing," Mayle said. "People really wanted to digest it."

Members Weigh the Deal

Lewis would later call it her "proudest moment." For the next two days, on sidewalks and plazas all over the city, instead of walking picket lines, teachers sat in circles reading and discussing the deal. Chants were replaced with murmurs and questions as teachers huddled in groups of three and four to peer over contract summaries.

At Emmet Elementary, "we sat down that Monday and we read through that huge document," said delegate Tammie Vinson. "Every school decided whether we wanted our delegate to go back and vote to accept it. We were able to ask questions and those questions were addressed."

The officers didn't go out and promote the deal. They were

CTU

Union members extended the strike to read the whole proposed contract together.

back in the negotiating room, cleaning up the unfinished language—and besides, it wasn't their call. "I'm not going to say this is the greatest thing since sliced bread and try to sell it to them. I'm not a marketer," said Lewis. "Our people know how to read, they know how to do math, and they understand these things."

Ashby, who volunteered to help deliver the strike newsletters to picket sites that day, was moved at the sight of the impromptu study circles. "Think about what percentage of an average union's members have read the entire contract," he said. "It's miniscule. We now have a situation where 99 percent of a union's membership read every single word of that contract. And they debated it: 'Did we win enough for the parents? For our students? If we stay out on strike, can we win more?' It was a total exercise in democracy."

At the end of the two days, the delegates met again. In a voice vote, they overwhelmingly chose to suspend the strike, sending the contract back to members for ratification. Members ratified it two weeks later, with 79 percent voting yes.

Emanuel's school board head Jean-Claude Brizard fell on his sword when the strike ended, and resigned. A year later he said in an interview, "We severely underestimated the ability of the Chicago Teachers Union to lead a massive grassroots campaign against our administration. It's a lesson for all of us in the reform community."

Lessons

⇨ CTU didn't ask parents and the public to support the strike as a one-off event. The union made it clear that all the union's battles—for a "better school day," for money for schools, against school closings, and finally the contract campaign and strike—

were part of the same fight for public education and workers' rights.

⇨ Months before the strike began, CTU recruited and trained a network of strike captains and coordinators covering every school. Members' experiences in public outreach and protests prior to the strike helped prepare them for daily activities during the strike.

⇨ Union leaders struck a balance, making sure a few essential strike activities, such as picket-line roll call, daily debrief, and mass rallies, happened in coordination across the city, while leaving room for members to improvise activities at their schools and neighborhoods. Strikers and supporters made the strike their own by bringing creativity, local issues, and local flair to their picket lines.

⇨ Instead of assigning different days for each member to picket, CTU asked all members to be on the lines every morning, and join the big rally every afternoon. The high participation helped strikers stay united and upbeat.

⇨ The immense outpouring of community support for the strike was the fruit of years of collaboration. Still, part of picket duty was canvassing parents in the neighborhoods, to continue to build support and to battle the anti-union messages coming from politicians, the board, and media.

⇨ CTU made sure aid from the national union came without strings attached, and kept local control of bargaining.

⇨ Strikers experienced new levels of power and freedom from fear, permanently strengthening their participation in the union.

⇨ Delegates chose to invite the whole membership to take part in the decision whether to end the strike. This democratic process ensured members felt ownership of the deal, including its compromises.

⇨ CTU educated members that the strike was just one battle in a longer war for public education. This helped to keep them from feeling burned when the strike didn't fix all their problems and when CPS closed 47 schools the next year.

10

What They Won

Everyone agrees that CTU won the 2012 strike. Mayor Rahm Emanuel's heavy-handed tactics backfired, and he had to retreat, compromise, and then campaign to save face. In a bizarre turn, the mayor put out a post-strike TV ad to convince the public what he'd achieved. The million-dollar ad was paid for by the anti-teacher group Education Reform Now.

CTU won in the court of public opinion, which affirmed not just the union's right to defend teachers' conditions but also the union's whole approach to defending public education. The union did such a good job of articulating what was wrong with Chicago schools—and exactly how they could be fixed—that many observers thought the strike was primarily about smaller class sizes.

In a sense, it was, along with all the other improvements students needed. As described in Chapter 9, Chicago teachers could legally bargain over "mandatory" subjects such as pay and benefits, but only over "permissive" subjects such as class sizes if the board of education agreed. The union could not legally strike over a permissive subject.

Said Staff Coordinator Jackson Potter, "We had to be careful about explaining our reasons for striking. We could say 'we want this changed' but we couldn't say 'we're striking over this.' The district tries to set the stage for an injunction if they need one"—that is, to stop the strike if the district could "prove" to a judge that the strike was over a permissive subject.

"It was a constant tug of war," Potter said, "that limited our ability to articulate our reasons for fighting so hard."

That disadvantage was not so apparent to Chicago residents, however, who had been convinced by CTU's actions over the previous two years that the union was all about conditions for students.

In the end, the district agreed to talk about class size—calling the existing language "outdated"—but what the union won, Potter said, "wasn't enough." The last three contracts had included guidelines on class size limits, and those were retained: 28 for kindergarten through fifth grade, 31 for higher grades. Also maintained was a "monitoring panel" made up of retired principals and teachers that can investigate schools with egregiously large classes. The panel can recommend changes in programming at the school or the distribution of students, to even out class sizes, and even has a pot of a half-million dollars to hire more staff.

But once that money is gone, there is no contractual way for the union to force the district to address overcrowded classes. The 2012 contract added language that a parent chosen by the Local School Council will be added to the panel at a school under investigation. "It will help us expose the problem," said Financial Secretary Kristine Mayle, "but not necessarily fix it."

When it came to other aspects of working conditions, teachers nationwide were elated to see someone resisting the tide of corporate-backed concessions that teachers have accepted in recent years, in particular merit pay and evaluations based on student test scores (see the Appendix).

Union leaders say a big part of their victory was simply holding the line on longstanding aspects of their contract and fending off givebacks. The board at first proposed a thin, 24-page contract (the old contract was 300 pages). And leaders are proud of their victory on the longer school day (Chapter 7), which won 512 additional jobs and was inked two months before the strike.

Otherwise, the contract was not chock-full of big improvements. Rather, in many areas CTU won defensive victories—the school board had to back down on aggressive proposals that had been won in other cities, or settle for half a loaf.

The contract was a victory for students in that it will help experienced teachers to stay in the classroom, rather than allowing principals to dismiss them willy-nilly. But it did not address— because it could not—many issues of direct impact on students, in particular school closings. The union was left to fight on those issues in other ways. And as the 2012-2013 school year demonstrated (see Chapter 11), many gains could be overturned, in practice, through massive closings and layoffs.

What They Won

Merit Pay: The board wanted merit pay tied to evaluations instead of the "lanes and steps" system that rewarded longevity and advanced degrees with higher pay. Merit pay was a top goal of Emanuel (and of corporate education interests nationwide). CTU kept the lanes, based on education, and steps, based on length of service, and fended off merit pay completely.

Evaluations: The board wanted to require that 45 percent of each evaluation be based on student test scores, the maximum allowed by state law. Teachers say this method is part of the "blame the teacher" scapegoating for the woeful state of public education. Such ratings can be erratic, showing a teacher's effectiveness as high one year and low the next, and can have high margins of error. And, of course, it's not possible to isolate an individual teacher's input from all other factors affecting student performance, such as income level, family situation, health, or even a child's state of mind on test day.

In addition, the union had always had problems with the evaluations made by principals. "Plenty of principals use evaluations to get rid of teachers who challenge them," said social studies teacher Bill Lamme, "or they want to hire their brother-in-law. There are lots of bad principals who think their job is to purge experienced teachers. Those are the ones most likely to challenge any new b.s. plans coming down. The principals want younger, malleable teachers. The massacre of experienced teachers is not just about money but about institutional memory."

CTU kept the percentage of each evaluation to be based on test scores to 25, the minimum requirement under Illinois law, rising to 30 percent in the contract's last year. The other 70 percent of evaluation will be done by principals or their designees. But teachers will now be able to appeal their evaluations, a right they didn't have before. Mid-year evaluations, which principals often used to oust teachers, were disallowed.

The union has some hope that a new framework for evaluations, the Charlotte Danielson system, will be more objective than the old checklists.

Layoff Rights: Before the Renaissance 2010 plan, layoffs had been rare, and laid-off teachers had no rights to be rehired at all. Now, because of Emanuel's wave of school closings, layoffs are rampant. The new language says that if a school closes, teachers—by a combination of seniority, evaluation rating, and their areas of expertise—can follow the students to their new schools. This right could help slow the loss of black teachers, the ones overwhelmingly affected by the shutdown of black schools. In a non-closing situation, a laid-off teacher has 10 months of recall rights to her same school.

In exchange, the union gave up some pay and rights for laid-off teachers. In the past, they could spend 40 weeks as a substitute assigned to one school, at full salary and benefits. Now, they will have 20 weeks in that situation and 20 weeks as a day-to-day substitute, sent to different schools, with benefits but lower pay.

Teachers with "unsatisfactory" or "needs improvement" ratings will be laid off before those with higher ratings, although non-tenured teachers will go first. CPS had already unilaterally implemented this change in 2010 and the courts had agreed.

Rehire Rights: When principals hire for the coming year, at least half of those newly hired must come from the pool of displaced teachers. If at least three teachers from the pool apply for a particular job, the principal must hire one of them, or justify her action.

The new hiring pool has weaknesses, however. Those rated "excellent" or "proficient" will be in the pool automatically, but lower-rated teachers must get two letters of recommendation from people who have observed them teaching and hold an interview with an administrator. It may be easier for new college graduates to get into the pool than teachers with "unsatisfactory" ratings.

Fall 2013 would have been the testing period for the new pool and the "follow your students" rights—but the magnitude of closings and layoffs (see Chapter 11) challenged implementation of the new system.

Recruitment of Black and Latino teachers: The board committed to making a plan to search for and recruit racially diverse teachers and to retrain principals and administrators about the plan, and to share data with CTU. This clause was designed to address the disproportionate effect of school closings and layoffs on black teachers in particular.

Raises: Teachers won 3 percent the first year (4 percent for paraprofessionals) and 2 percent in each of the last two years of the contract.

Discipline: CTU improved the procedure, eliminating unpaid suspensions. For the first time, a mediation-arbitration process would allow a neutral third-party to weigh in on disciplinary matters and the third party's decision would be binding. The union also secured just-cause provisions for the first time.

Health Benefits: Members saw no increases to insurance premiums or co-pays, but an unpopular "wellness program" was introduced, part of a national trend designed to shift insurance costs from employers to employees. Members and covered spouses must fill out an assessment and take five free biometric tests, such as cholesterol. Based on the results, they are hooked up with a coach.

Members must also earn points each month by logging onto a wellness website to read articles or watch videos for 15 minutes. They're fined $50 per month if they don't do so, or if they don't take the biometric tests, but there are no fines for failing to reach wellness goals set by the coach.

Special Education: Violations of state or federal law regarding special education—such as exceeding class size limits or not getting an assistant—are frequent. They can now be grieved.

Clinicians: Nurses and social workers won basic rights like private meeting space, locked cabinets, and access to printers.

Other: Students are guaranteed to get their books on the first day of school. A $250 reimbursement to teachers for supplies, up from $100. Break time for nursing mothers. Paternity leave. The board agreed to hire more social workers, counselors, psychologists, and school nurses, but only if new sources of revenue were found—and unsurprisingly, that has not happened.

Another gain: this contract lasts three years instead of four. "That way it has to be redone when the mayor is trying to run for reelection," district supervisor Andrea Parker pointed out.

Community organizer Jitu Brown, who'd worked with CTU leaders since the CORE days, put the strike and the contract in perspective. "This fight was not going to be won in the seven days that there was a teachers' strike," he said. "What we did get was activation of a sleeping giant. Now we've got the CTU on alert and a union that's got the capacity to tap into its base. And that base is not depressed, not scattered. They organized their base to move. That's one thing that definitely came out of it."

After the strike, Debby Pope worked on fielding the many speaking requests from unions—and not just teachers unions— around the country. She saw firsthand how badly others wanted to learn from the CTU experience, and how inspired they were.

Pope assists with contract implementation as a Grievance Department staffer, so she's seen the contract's warts and beauty marks. "We made some gains in some areas, we lost some things in other areas, but overall, we have a better contract for having done the strike," she said. "And even if we didn't have a significantly better contract, we have a much better union."

After they signed the contract, CTU leaders and rank and filers barely had time to breathe before the next act of aggression from the mayor and the school board. Chapter 11 will summarize how the newly strengthened union went on to tackle its next set of challenges.

Lessons

⇨ CTU pressed on "permissive subjects" to the max, using every available forum in addition to the bargaining table to make gains in areas that management was not legally required to bargain over.

⇨ CTU maintained a bedrock union principle against management favoritism by rejecting merit pay.

⇨ CTU looked ahead to the school closings that were clearly coming and aimed to protect members with new language on recall rights.

⇨ The contract itself was a mixed bag—but the union and its community allies won in the court of public opinion, and the strike strengthened them for the battles to come.

11

Maintaining Momentum

At the height of the strike, CTU had thousands of people in the streets of Chicago, a sea of red shirts marching through downtown, and national attention. But the contract settlement itself was mixed.

The concessions could have deflated members who had felt incredibly powerful as they shut the school system down for nine days and put their education politics on the front pages. And after teachers settled back into their classrooms, the union was still faced with looming school closings, growth of charter schools, and all the aggressive attacks on public education. How would Chicago teachers sustain their activism when they returned to school?

At an event debriefing the strike, Staff Coordinator Jackson Potter described the importance of the post-strike period—one that would define, he said, "whether we have more victories or we fall on our faces. We really have to figure out the next steps to not allow this moment to dissipate."

Financial Secretary Kristine Mayle credits the ratification process itself with keeping members engaged and loyal to the union in the post-strike period. "Before it was ratified by the membership, we did a ton of school meetings," she said. These meetings were a stark contrast to how leaders had treated previous settlements. "In the past those would have been the meetings where you try to sell the contract. We had an honest conversation: 'Here's all the great stuff we got. Here's what we got that's not so great.'

"Some people got angry, we got yelled at, but on the whole, people understood."

Not Defensive

The delegates' and other leaders' willingness to listen—and members' ability to make themselves heard and produce democratic solutions—came into play at Curie High School in spring 2013. Teachers there were furious that the contract's language on maternity leave was not as good as they thought officers had led them to believe. The language was broad, without details, and CPS was being neither upfront nor clear. Details had not been published till some women had already decided their timeline for getting pregnant.

The Curie delegate arranged a conference call with Jackson Potter and Kristine Mayle. After some initial dressing down on the part of the members, the leaders admitted that their concerns were quite valid. The teachers wanted a statement from the union within two weeks explaining the maternity leave provisions.

Potter suggested, "Why don't we do it together? So we don't post it and it's still not adequate." The teachers agreed and a thorough, accurate statement was jointly hammered out and put on the CTU website. ✿

Leaders knew they would have to keep both the school-level and the district-wide fights going. Mayle said it was not easy. "People were exhausted," she recalled in summer 2013. "Last year was really hard on people: the strike, the lead-up, but also the longer day, Rahm…the internal school committees died off a bit, but delegates are still informed and knowing what's happening."

To maintain the union presence in the schools, leaders encouraged members to keep wearing red on Fridays and members of the Contract Action Committees to stay active at their schools. "The wearing of the red still continues to this day," reported delegate Kimberly Bowsky a year after the strike. "The majority of educators in my building wear red every Friday… Even kids go, 'Where's your red, Ms. Bowsky?' The one or two times I forgot, my colleagues gave me a real hard time. These were people who did not see themselves as union people before."

Leaders also worked to beef up the elected Professional Problems Committees (see Chapter 5) that assist the delegates and meet monthly with the principals to resolve issues, so members could use them to enforce the new contract themselves in their buildings.

Organizers went to schools to help set up the PPCs and develop an agenda for dealing with the principal. "The ideal is to have fewer grievances written," Organizing Director Norine Gutekanst said, "with the goal that the principal backs down."

"The big change in terms of delegates," said Mayle, "is that people are starting to mentor their potential replacements before they step down. Before, they would just quit and leave a mess behind and schools would be left with a new delegate that was not yet trained or prepared. Now the 'retiring' delegates are bringing their potential replacements to House meetings and showing them the ropes of the job. They've also been more open to letting the younger teachers take the lead."

Union committees have also grown, adding members who weren't involved before the strike. On the special education committee, Mayle said, "some are younger, but most, a surprising number, are older teachers that had given up hope and seem to have gotten some back."

Fight against School Closings

Beyond contract enforcement, teachers knew they were facing a bigger fight than ever over the future of public schools, with Emanuel determined to weaken and shrink the union, close schools, and expand charters. So a second goal for the delegates

---

Victory against Turnaround

When Clara Barton Elementary was placed on CPS's "turnaround" list in 2013, kindergarten teacher Phyllis Trottman, who was a delegate and district supervisor, and parent Sonya Williams, chair of the Local School Council, sprang into action.

They got in touch with community organizations and their state representative, state senator, and alderman. They raised money for two buses to send parents to speak at a school board meeting downtown, wearing "Barton School" shirts.

When the board held a hearing on the turnaround (though no one from the board actually attended), 200 parents and students filled the room. "I brought a kindergartner to read 'Chicken Little,'" Trottman said. "We were letting them know Barton is not the type of school you would need to turn around."

CTU sponsored buses to a second board meeting. And when the board issued its final list of turnarounds and closings, Barton was saved. ✿

and committees was to
get into the campaigns
against school closings.

After the contract
was settled, rumors be-
gan to spread that the
board would close as
many as 100 schools.
The new CEO, Barbara
Byrd-Bennett, delayed
the inevitable confron-
tation by extending till
March the December 1
deadline to announce
the closures. The district
told the public it would
do a big round of clos-
ings, then commit to five
years with none.

But CTU called for a moratorium. The union continued
training delegates to take a big-picture approach, and throughout the 2012-2013 school year made the closings a citywide fight,
rather than a school-by-school battle. It devoted most of its organizing department to the campaign and did massive member
education, including mailings, calls, and visits. School and neighborhood meetings were called to involve parents and community
groups; the bonds with parents forged before and during the strike
carried over into protests around the city and at hearings set up by
the district.

Activists held a November 2012 sit-in at City Hall to protest
potential closings; 10 were arrested when they refused to leave
without being allowed to speak to the mayor. CTU didn't even
have to take the lead; the action was organized by Teachers for
Social Justice, Action Now, Albany Park Neighborhood Council,
and Kenwood Oakland Community Organization.

The CTU Research Department issued a report in late November, a follow-up to the earlier *The Schools Chicago's Students
Deserve*. Detailing the stark racial inequality in the schools, *The
Black and White of Education in Chicago's Public Schools* (online at
bit.ly/Black-White-Report) laid out how, since 1995, corporate "re-

formers" had replaced public schools with privately run charters, increased emphasis on testing, displaced African American teachers, and starved schools of resources. The result, CTU said, was increasing class sizes, racial segregation, displacement of students, and punitive student discipline. The board's moves had lessened opportunities for deeper conceptual learning, depleted stable African American neighborhood schools in particular, and promoted disrespect and poor treatment of teachers by blaming them for underperforming schools.

The report was introduced at a heated press conference where, said Mayle, the union "really called out the board for racism. It's something that everybody in Chicago knows," she said—but CTU backed it up with research. "They can't deny it."

Escalating the Citywide Fight

In March, the city announced a staggering number of closures, the most ever in a single year in Chicago or any other U.S. city, 54 elementary schools. "The only thing that's like it is Hurricane Katrina," said Vice President Jesse Sharkey of the potential devastation, "except this is being done on purpose."

Almost all the closings targeted black and Latino schools, affecting around 30,000 students. Fifty were on the West and South Sides, in poor neighborhoods. By the summer, layoffs of school employees had reached 3,100.

Officials used "school utilization" meetings and PowerPoint presentations to try to win parents over to support their schools' being closed. Nearly a half-million dollars from Walmart's charity, the Walton Family Foundation, paid for a marketing agency to set up focus-group-style sessions.

Students spoke out at a community hearing on closing Crane High School.

A city hall sit-in against school closings.

But in many hearings (which were required by law), officials could not execute their plans. Community members attending the more than 40 hearings voiced overwhelming opposition. CTU estimated as many as 20,000 parents and teachers showed up to the hearings and related events, to insist they wanted no schools closed.

A February 2013 hearing in the Pilsen neighborhood, for instance, overflowed with shouting and protesting parents. They refused to participate in the break-out sessions, preferring to speak up in the large auditorium setting. Similar scenes took place in the Logan Square and Uptown neighborhoods.

"Parents are leading the way," said CTU organizer Brandon Johnson. "It's spreading like wildfire." But "the challenge we face is that the actual decision-makers are insulated from democratic decision-making," Sharkey noted.

No one made this more evident than Mayor Rahm Emanuel, off on a skiing holiday when the closings were announced. Byrd-Bennett added to the tone-deaf response, saying there was "incredible support" for the closings in the affected communities, and even calling her plan evidence that CPS officials were "actually listening to parents."

A March 27 action brought thousands of teachers and community activists to City Hall. The rally was large and spirited, though it failed to match the numbers at the height of the contract campaign the year before. In May, a three-day march covered 18 miles through the South and West Sides; 100 people took part in each of various stages as they traveled through communities to Daley Plaza. Twenty-six were arrested at a City Hall sit-in where they blocked elevators and sang protest songs from the civil rights movement.

The protests ultimately stopped only four closings and postponed three, leaving 47 schools to close. The forces arrayed against CTU proved too powerful to overcome that year. But the union showed Chicago's elite that "no one is going to shut up and

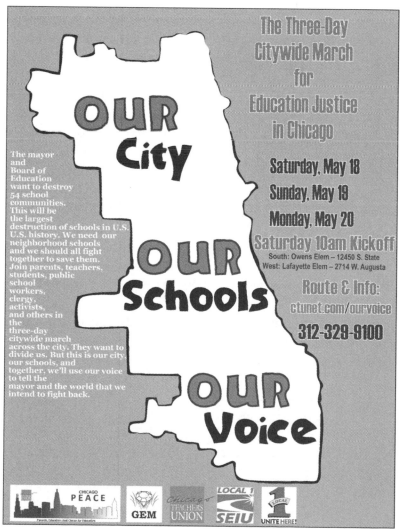

go away," Johnson said. "You are going to see the same things as last year: more protests that will be larger, more teach-ins, larger caravans to lobby on behalf of educational justice."

"People bank on a level of unconcern: as long as my family or my community is okay I don't care about anyone else's," said Tammy Vinson, who now teaches at Oscar DePriest Elementary after her school closed. "But I think CTU showed you cannot be unconcerned. You cannot keep things contained. If you don't believe communities kept disadvantaged and starving are going to impact you and your community, you're clueless. You cannot sweep people under the rug and not believe people are going to come out."

"If we build a large enough movement," said Sharkey, referring to protest tactics of the civil rights movement and the 1960s, "we can provoke a real political crisis in the city. Then the mayor is going to have to figure out what he is going to do."

While continuing to fight the privatization of education, CTU members were also supporting organizing under the noses of their antagonists, the charter school operators. Since 2008, teachers at 12 charter schools had joined a special charter-school local of the American Federation of Teachers (AFT)—creating the possibility of bringing together two groups of workers usually pitted against each other.

Teachers at 13 more schools, from the UNO charter school chain, joined the union in 2013. CTU provided an organizer for the campaign and established a rank-and-file committee of teachers to support charter organizing. Apparently CTU's polarizing strike hadn't turned non-union teachers away from the labor movement; in fact, perhaps it inspired them.

Keeping CORE Active

After the strike, the CORE caucus grew. Its monthly meetings in 2013 drew as many as 100. "CORE was integral in getting thousands of parents and teachers to the school closing meetings," elementary school teacher Nate Rasmussen said.

CORE sponsored a national conference in August 2013 to build a network of teachers who wanted to make their unions "instruments in the fight for social justice." Teachers from both the AFT and the NEA were invited to come in delegations of three to six—the better to implement lessons learned back home.

As a caucus, CORE could reach out to both local officers and rank and filers, incumbents and oppositionists, without worrying about formal or informal relationships CTU had with other locals.

The conference discussed how to build democratic locals through current leadership structures or new caucuses, how to build parent/community alliances, and how to fight on education issues such as high-stakes testing. Workshops discussed the basics of organizing (how to get parents involved, how to talk to your co-workers, how to run for office) and the bottom-line question: "How do we combine bread-and-butter union issues with social justice and educational justice?"

Logan Square Neighborhood Association attended a CPS school closing hearing, February 2013.

Sarah Jane Rhee, loveandstrugglephotos.com

One workshop was on research. It turned out that a half-dozen teacher groups were working on reports similar to *The Schools Chicago's Students Deserve* for their own cities.

In May, CORE faced reelection for the top offices of CTU. "We didn't want to take anything for granted," said steering committee member Sarah Chambers, who led the get-out-the-vote campaign. So CORE first established its support by gathering 10,000 signatures, well above the number required to run a slate.

The campaign committee divided the district into five regions, with a leader in charge of each. Each CORE activist was asked to leaflet three schools. They raised money for mailings and campaign materials and set up a media committee for emails, the website, and to design posters and flyers.

Following the template of their original campaign for union office (and their experience with the strike vote), the campaigners rigorously tracked their support by school and region, up till election day. (See Chapter 4 for details of CORE's first campaign for office and some tips from their 2013 reelection campaign.)

"A big part of these campaigns," Chambers said, "is finding leaders and building leaders. Some of the regional leaders will be on the CORE steering committee. We are building them up, mak-

ing the second and third layers of CORE." After the vote, CORE meetings continued to be large, even over the summer, and the caucus began regional meetings again to allow more participation.

"Just because we have some people in leadership who are at the union offices, that's no reason for us to breathe a sigh of relief," said Bowsky. "It's not over and it's not won... One of the things we have to worry about is taking stock of our forces—constantly making sure people are involved, that we're adding to our ranks."

National Impact

The Chicago teachers strike was a shot in the arm to teachers across the country, an example of resistance in a time when public sector unions had been in retreat.

In particular, the strike cut across the grain of both the national teachers unions. The AFT has promoted conciliatory relationships with urban school districts like Chicago's in recent years. The union has agreed to major concessions, including merit pay, in New Haven, Newark, Cleveland, and Baltimore, and promoted what President Randi Weingarten calls "solution-based unionism." The National Education Association has also collaborated, on issues such as changing teacher evaluation and implementing Common Core standards, with corporate reformers like Bill Gates.

In Chicago, though, the strength of the local organizing compelled the national union to respect CTU's autonomy and support the strike, and even led it to ride the wave of popularity after the fact—despite the fact that CTU's strategy was starkly different from what the AFT endorsed in other cities.

The ripple effects of the strike could be seen right away. That fall, seven Chicago-area districts followed with strikes of their own. Before the CTU strike, only one school district in the area had gone on strike since 2004.

CTU also showed other public sector workers how to exert power differently than by traditional lobbying and political endorsements. State workers in AFSCME Illinois, who had never struck, were inspired by CTU. Suddenly their union leaders began preparing members for the possibility of a strike, though they avoided it with an eleventh-hour settlement.

Leaders from CORE also worked informally with teachers in Philadelphia, St. Paul, Seattle, and a dozen other districts to share strategies about mobilizing members and community.

Teacher Uprisings

In Newark and New York City, caucuses inspired by Chicago sprung up, hoping to take on stagnant and entrenched leaders with an alternative to the damage-control approach and to closed-door negotiating.

A year after incumbents negotiated a contract that included merit pay, the Newark Education Workers (NEW) caucus campaigned against the concessions and pledged to build a CTU-model union. NEW won a majority of seats on the executive board and almost took the presidential spot, losing by nine votes.

Activists in Massachusetts formed the statewide coalition Educators for a Democratic Union after the Massachusetts Teachers Association cooperated with Democratic legislators to pass a law weakening teacher job security. They convened a statewide conference, with a CORE leader as guest speaker, to discuss plans to run a slate in the next election.

In Hawaii, teachers at a suburban high school organized a work-to-rule protest of an imposed contract. Through social media and grassroots promotion, the action spread across the state, with more than 100 schools participating. Support from parents and the community gave bargaining traction to union officers; the rank and filers "led from the back of the room," as CORE once had.

In Portland, Oregon, teachers followed CTU's campaign closely and met with CTU leaders. When their time to bargain came, their proposal included "The Schools Portland Students Deserve," including smaller classes and more resources in high-poverty schools and a pushback against standardized tests.

In Los Angeles, teachers, parents, and community groups formed a coalition called The Schools Los Angeles Students Deserve. They protested a costly plan to give students iPads preprogrammed with testing material and organized against excessive testing and for better use of technology.

Rank-and-file teachers at a Seattle high school announced in January 2013 they were boycotting a district-mandated stan-

Anna Schneide ; Insideschools.org

Teachers and parents refused to let kindergartners at Castle Bridge Elementary in New York City be tested.

dardized test called the MAP, which they said was arbitrary and counterproductive for students. Their "Scrap the Map" campaign generated national attention and support. The teachers planned their action without their local union leaders, but after they went public, the local union and the national NEA decided to support the boycott. The district initially threatened to punish the teachers, but finally backed down and made the test optional for high school students.

In October that year, parents at Castle Bridge Elementary in New York City opted out of a new state-mandated exam for students in kindergarten through second grade. One of the parents was an activist in a teachers caucus modeled after CORE, and teachers aided the effort while parents were out in front. When 80 percent of parents refused to let their kids—as young as four years old—take the test, the principal canceled it, saying that in addition to being bad for the children, it was an unfair measurement of their teachers.

Like the Chicago strikers, the anti-test teachers in Seattle and New York disrupted the corporate agenda both as workers and as educators. They highlighted how standardized tests, which more and more are used to attack teachers' pay and job security, are also harmful to students' learning. In November 2013, following

the lead of teachers and parents who were already pushing on the issue, CTU took up the anti-testing drive with a campaign to "Let Us Teach!"

The national AFT and NEA have made changes in part influenced by CTU's model. Noting the success of CTU's community work, the AFT began urging other locals to find community partners; sometimes it has sent staff to help local efforts. In Philadelphia, where the union was facing attacks as grave as Chicago's, AFT supported work with the Philadelphia Coalition Advocating for Public Schools. Both unions held national conferences where community leaders could strategize with teacher locals.

Challenging the Billionaires' Agenda

Before, during, and since the strike, CTU's challenge to the national corporate education agenda has gained a foothold. Although the billionaire-backed groups and their politician allies are as aggressive as ever, another story about how schools are failing—and how to fix them—is now available to anyone who wants to hear it.

CTU has exposed, if not stopped, the shadowy corporate interests invested in privatizing and monetizing public education—the American Legislative Exchange Council (ALEC), the hedge funds, Democrats for Education Reform—and the corporate self-interest behind self-styled do-gooders like Stand for Children. (See the Appendix for more on all of these groups.)

The bad guys have taken some hits in the public eye; for instance, CTU publicized a cynical video of Stand for Children's Jonah Edelman bragging about anti-teacher legislation, which became an embarrassment and wrung an apology from Edelman. At CPS school closing hearings, Chicago reporters identified paid pro-closing participants who were eventually linked back to Mayor Emanuel through his longtime political consulting firm.

The union also helped publicize a corruption scandal in the UNO charter school chain—run by Emanuel advisor Juan Rangel—involving self-dealing and contracts to relatives. The scandal helped the AFT's charter school local win organizing ground rules for teachers at every school in the chain. All 13 campuses then went union.

Even nationally, the promise that closing schools will miraculously increase test scores is being viewed more skeptically—at least in some circles. More and more people know that charter schools' results do not exceed those of public schools. The feature film "Won't Back Down," about public school parents fighting a corrupt teachers union, was a box-office flop.

That said, the corporate offensive has not slowed. Unembarrassed by scandals or statistics, proponents of profitable privatization continue to press CTU, while the union bolsters its alliances for the next round.

Reelection

Chicago media flocked to cover the opposition candidates in the May 2013 CTU election, predicting that the Coalition to Save Our Union caucus could give Karen Lewis and the CORE slate a run for their money. Instead, leaders were reelected with a resounding 80 percent of the vote.

The election was a referendum on CORE's efforts to raise teachers' expectations and resist the attack on education. The opposition claimed CORE leaders had shouted in the streets rather than being savvy at the bargaining table. They criticized the concessions made in the contract and spread the message that "you poked the bear": that CTU's militancy brought on retaliation in the form of school closings.

But CORE was re-energized by the test. Leaders did not want to just eke out a win; they wanted a strong showing from a wide base. The results were an endorsement, not just of popular leaders, but of a vision for what a union should be—and a strategy for what it should do. As Gutekanst said, "It showed the members want a fighting union."

Lessons

⇨ CTU was not complacent after the strike but used its momentum to battle school closings.

⇨ CTU didn't impose an agenda on community partners. At each school threatened with closing, teachers met with parents and community members to devise strategies together.

⇨ Leaders weren't defensive about contract shortcomings, but engaged disgruntled members in fixing problems.

⇨ CORE members sought a big reelection victory as a mandate to continue their work; in the process, they re-energized CORE and developed new leaders.

⇨ CORE met with teacher activists in other cities to share Chicago's lessons and help ignite the battle against the corporate reformers nationally.

12

Lessons

It's happened time and again: Reformers take over at the union hall. They're sick of seeing management run roughshod over their local, so they put together a slate and a plan to mobilize the members. When it works, reformers can transform dormant locals, channel union power into grassroots hands, and put management on notice.

But too often reformers fail. Either they don't accomplish much and they get voted out, or they do achieve something but fail to involve members, and still get the boot. Too many don't know how to step off the path of least resistance, so they slide into the well-worn grooves of their predecessors—and members don't see enough change.

We asked two teachers who'd been with CORE since the very beginning how CORE and the new leaders were able to get so many members involved. Why was CORE's experience different from that of other reformers who wanted to mobilize members to take on management, but weren't able to? For that matter, why was their public support so much greater than that of other public employees who've struck to defend their conditions?

Al Ramirez, who teaches elementary school, said CORE encountered a "perfect storm." "One, we had the perfect villain—Rahm Emanuel. Two, we had a lot of smart, hard-working people. And three, teachers were working under horrible conditions and they reached the boiling point."

Of course, lots of caucuses are made up of smart people, and there are plenty of management villains out there, who all create horrible conditions. Ramirez continued, "We tried to build a base inside every school and a Contract Action Committee in every school. We always started with 'what are our issues here in this school?' and connected them to the contract fight.

"Plus we made lots of opportunities for people to get involved." Members could choose their level of involvement. "You could go leafleting or have an informational picket in your community. And people were expected to reach out to parents."

Norine Gutekanst, who became CTU's organizing director, added, "We gave them the information to use with parents about why what the board wanted was bad for the kids. For members who hadn't cared so much about the union piece—well, they did care about the kids. Now the union could be a way to fight for them, too.

"And we talked about how racist the school system was. Anyone who worked in a black or brown community, they felt it or knew it, but it hadn't been given voice before.

"Our members were always butting their heads up against the system. What we did freed them to say, 'My kids are getting shortchanged, and I'm getting shortchanged, and it's the system that's the problem.'"

It's worth adding that CORE wasn't organized primarily as an electoral vehicle or around a single candidate. CORE's critique of the union leadership grew out of its criticisms of management and the whole educational system in Chicago. By putting those ideas into action even before taking office, CORE was able to make the union election a referendum on strategy and on competing visions of the union, rather than an apolitical "who can make the trains the run on time?"

○

The CTU experience allows us to say:

It's Possible to Confront the Austerity Agenda. Public employees in city after city have fallen victim to politicians' cry of "tighten your belts." But instead of accepting the idea that there is no alternative to austerity, CTU went after the folks with deep pockets.

With its community allies, CTU used direct action and creative tactics to confront corporations and the 1%, to demonstrate with word and deed that there is plenty of money out there for schools. It's just in the wrong hands.

By the time of the strike, CTU members and parents weren't swayed by the argument that "there is no alternative to cuts." They were on the side of CTU.

It's Possible to Confront the Wall Street Democrats. President Karen Lewis has said, "In education, we don't have political allies we can count on. It's one place Democrats and Republicans can agree."

The kind of confrontation represented by the strike wasn't supposed to happen. Rahm Emanuel swept into the mayor's office like a force of nature. Most of Chicago's union leaders were afraid of getting crushed by President Obama's former chief of staff.

It was also a presidential election year. A strike would be a black eye for the president, the union's foes chided, and could cost him his reelection. But CTU took on the city, state, and national Democratic establishments, on an issue that unites today's Democratic (and Republican) politicians almost unanimously—school reform. By the time they were through, Emanuel had overreached and looked desperate, and the implications for Obama were a non-issue.

CTU managed almost singlehandedly to turn the common sense about school reform on its head. The debate was no longer about merit pay and getting rid of "bad teachers"; it was about air conditioning and books for students on the first day of school, access to art and world language teachers, and why all the schools targeted for closure were in black and Latino neighborhoods.

Sarah Jane Rhee, loveandstrugglephotos.com

Speaking Out about "Educational Apartheid" Struck a Nerve. CTU didn't shy away from making the strike about racial justice, going so far as to call the CPS system Exhibit A for educational apartheid. By giving voice to an unspoken truth many parents knew, they positioned the union as a passionate champion of the public interest, not a defender of the status quo. As a result, parents trusted the teachers more than the mayor—because the teachers called it like it was.

Leaders Trusted Members to Grow through Their Experiences. Making an issue of the dramatic loss of African American teachers, and the racism of the schools in general, could have been controversial among CTU's white members. It took time, but support for this issue grew. Leaders knew that action opens minds, and they actively wanted to raise consciousness and build a common core of beliefs. The union's organizing for racial justice had as big an impact on its own members as it did on the community as a whole.

It's Possible to Fight for Bread and Butter and the Big Picture at the Same Time. The union made it clear, not just at contract time but for the two years prior, that its members were fighting for the students, not just for their own conditions. As important, CTU made clear how dumping on teachers and turning classrooms into a revolving door for inexperienced teachers would worsen students' lot, not improve it.

CTU showed that fighting against contract concessions and fighting for community demands were two sides of the same coin. Both sets of issues were forced on students and teachers by the same corporate forces for the same reasons. At a moment when the world was being told that greedy unions were the cause of budget problems, instead community allies were convinced that a strong union was part of the solution.

The union's message to members and allies was clear: teachers and students are not competing with each other for resources and money. They are both competing with the bankers, billionaires, and politicians who drive and profit from the austerity agenda.

It's Possible to Raise Expectations and Aim High. Too many union leaders have spent the past 30 years managing labor's decline and lowering members' expectations. They have consistently aimed too low, both in estimating what members arc capable of and in figuring out what they could win. CTU leaders knew that members could organize themselves if given the tools and the go-ahead. And they refused to bargain against themselves by making preemptive concessions.

Leaders recognized that members could change if their expectations were raised. A few years ago CTU was not a union of thousands of militant, activist members. A majority didn't necessarily agree with all the arguments the CORE leaders put forth (scary tactics, issues that seemed "too radical," untested strategies like parent alliances). But those leaders argued for a clear vision and dove into democratic debate over the way forward, with faith that the members would come to the same conclusions they had.

Putting People Power to Work Requires Real Organizing, Not Just Mobilizing. Leaders got 90 percent of the members voting "yes" to strike, with hundreds of self-organized picket lines across the city—crossed by only a minuscule number of scabs—because they weren't just "doing turnout." They spent two years giving members the tools, structures, and space to do it themselves. Rank and filers did the heavy lifting—building relationships with co-workers and parents, charting their areas of strength and pockets of weakness, and ultimately moving fellow members into action.

Real organizing requires a lot more work on the front end, which the union's new leaders began immediately after taking office. (In fact, they began some of it even *before* taking office.) But it requires far less staff work on the back end, and exponentially expands what the union can accomplish.

Education Happens through Action. Members learned not just through union position papers or public forums but by engaging in struggles and experiences that gave them the confidence to demand more, dream bigger, take risks.

Union Democracy Made the Difference. The union's leadership had formed through a rank-and-file struggle to make their union into the organization they wanted it to be. Being a dissident caucus ensured plenty of debate and even discord, before and after they got elected. Once they got into office, they didn't tell everyone to go home and let them handle things. They pushed for more involvement, more debate, more discussion. Sometimes that debate was rough-and-tumble. Sometimes it took a lot of time.

But leaders recognized that, if you want people to take big risks and do big things, they have to own the decisions. They knew members were grown-ups, and grown-ups can tell when they're in charge and when they're not. Members' insistence on extending the strike by two days so they could review the proposals (see Chapter 9) showed that the rank and file realized something had changed.

Leaders also knew they would be under a lot of pressure to tone it down: bad advice from other labor leaders, threats from management, enduring union culture, legitimate fears about trying for something big and failing. CTU leaders knew that they needed the members to be demanding, in order to sustain their own bold instincts.

It's Possible to Buck Union Headquarters. On testing, evaluations, and merit pay, the national AFT was headed in a different direction from CTU. Yet CTU was able to have the strike it wanted, with the politics it wanted, because the local was so strong. AFT President Randi Weingarten knew when she was standing on stage in front of 7,000 fired-up members in May 2012 that she didn't want to try to get in their way. CTU leaders didn't just criticize the higher-ups but showed that they had an alternative strat-

egy that could move members and score victories.

A Strike Can Still Wield Power. This wasn't a symbolic strike. It was a far cry from one-day walkouts that serve more as protests than as sand in the gears. Members completely shut down the schools and disrupted everyday functioning for a big chunk of the city's residents, creating a political crisis the powers-that-be couldn't ignore.

At first blush public school teachers might seem to have no economic leverage. When they walk out, the district actually saves money, and working class parents are the ones inconvenienced. But crucially—thanks to CTU's track record—parents blamed the mayor, not the teachers, for the crisis, and that made it a crisis for him.

Public Employees Can Win Over the Public. Teachers may be better positioned than most to wins hearts and minds, but all public employees understand the ways their services are undermined by the bosses, the politicians, and business interests. The CTU experience shows that demanding a better system, and using the power of workers with collective bargaining rights to fight for the public interest, is a viable strategy. Making common cause with those who use public services, and positioning unionized employees as watchdogs of the public interest, wins support—unlike trying to fly under the radar and hoping no one notices public workers' pay and pensions.

It's Possible to Take Risks and Win. After CTU bargainers got a deal to bring 512 teachers back to work to cover the extra hours created by the longer school day—a major win on what Emanuel had made his signature issue—they could have settled the contract without a strike. It would have been safer. But leaders knew that in the long run they had to have a much more direct confrontation with the city's power structure. They had to engage in a riskier strategy and tackle riskier issues if they wanted a lasting victory.

It's a Marathon, Not a Sprint. CTU educated members that winning the battle for public education would take much more than a strike. And it's a good thing, because Rahm Emanuel didn't put his tail between his legs and slink offstage. He spent the next year shuttering a record 47 schools, the largest wave of school closings in the nation's history.

The closings were designed to demoralize and disorient the city's parents and teachers. But they embraced their own newfound militancy, reelecting the CORE slate by a 4 to 1 margin. The vote showed Emanuel hadn't made teachers regret their strike; he'd only shown them the need for a union with a fighting spirit and a plan to win.

Appendix

Understanding the Assault on Schools and Teachers

Teachers in the U.S. today face an incredibly hostile political landscape.

The showdown in Chicago pitted the Chicago Teachers Union against a high-powered national network of billionaires and politicians of both parties, who've spent decades and huge sums stacking the laws against teachers and making a blame-the-teacher ideology the conventional wisdom.

Here we examine why educators find themselves such a focus of animosity, tracing the national legislative and rhetorical attacks against them by Republicans, Democrats, foundations, private companies, and a complex of advocacy groups.

Pitting the Public against the Public Sector

Public sector workers have been the target of conservative politicians for decades, but since the 2008 financial meltdown they've also become a convenient scapegoat for what ails the economy.

Unfortunately, voters have been all too ready to believe that librarians and lunch ladies—and their modest pensions—are responsible for the tidal wave of red ink engulfing cities and states. As a result, most state and local governments have taken the ax to their budgets rather than reevaluate two generations of tax breaks they've given to corporations and the well-to-do.

The attacks on unionized public employees reached a fever pitch in 2010—just as reformers in the Caucus of Rank-and-File Educators took over CTU. Politicians across the political spectrum spent that election season campaigning against government employees, especially anyone with a union card in their pocket. They made a blunt, ugly appeal to workers angry about plummeting standards in the private sector—"You don't have a pension or health care, so why should the guy who takes your ticket on the turnpike?"

Riding the wave of insecurity and resentment stirred up by the Tea Party, conservatives took over statehouses and governor's mansions across the country. They wasted no time translating their union-busting campaign promises into legislation.

Two months into 2011, 18 states had introduced measures designed to clip public sector workers, proposing everything from the elimination of defined-benefit pensions to constitutional limits on the size of the government workforce. Fourteen had introduced "right-to-work" legislation, designed to weaken unions by allowing employees in a union workplace to pay neither dues nor a "fair share" fee. Maine's governor went so far as to remove labor history murals from state buildings, calling them "anti-business."

New Republican governors John Kasich in Ohio and Scott Walker in Wisconsin garnered national headlines with their campaigns to repeal collective bargaining rights for public employees. But the vigorous fightbacks in Wisconsin and Ohio marked the start of resistance to the conservative agenda, resistance that CTU's new leaders were determined to embrace and extend.

Teachers as Culprits

In all the scrutiny focused on public sector workers, teachers have felt the most heat. They're blamed for all the ills of public education.

State lawmakers have singled out teachers for a barrage of attacks beyond cutting pensions and pay. Their goal has been to replace traditional public schools with charters and to make it easier to get rid of teachers in the public schools that remain. This has meant undermining job security and tying teachers' evaluations to their students' test scores, as well as introducing competition through merit pay. Teachers unions are seen as the obstacles that keep this healthy competition among schools from proceeding smoothly.

As we detail below, the radical restructuring of how schools operate is the culmination of a coordinated onslaught against public education 20 years in the making, by a coalition of billionaires and ideologues.

From War on Poverty to War on Teachers

In the 1960s, as part of Lyndon Johnson's War on Poverty, the federal government's role in education was defined as ensuring equal access to educational opportunity. Federal tax dollars were directed to closing the achievement gap between poor and non-poor students, which stemmed primarily from the legacy of segregation. That meant hiring more teachers to reduce class sizes in poor communities—but it meant a lot more. School spending was just one part of an overall anti-poverty program that included public job creation, funding for affordable housing, and a stepped-up effort to eliminate hunger.

Together with Head Start, school breakfast and lunch programs, and desegregation, these initiatives had an impressive impact. The black-white achievement gap narrowed considerably through the 1970s and into the 1980s—until backlash against these programs, and against an active public sector more generally, led to budget cuts. Then progress on closing the achievement gap stalled out.

Although politicians frequently criticized public schools, it wasn't until 1994 that federal testing requirements were introduced. The Clinton administration tied aid for high-poverty schools to a requirement that states begin testing third- through eighth-graders annually in math and reading. By that time the social and economic programs of the Great Society were a distant memory. The government did little toward improving the lives of the poor anymore—except, supposedly, through education.

Spencer Tweedy

Testing requirements skyrocketed in 2001 with passage of the No Child Left Behind Act, spearheaded by the Bush Administration with bipartisan support. Framed as a civil rights initiative to ensure quality education for all, NCLB increased the frequency of testing and required states to break out student scores by race, gender, and socioeconomic status, with a goal that every student be proficient in the tested subjects of reading, math, and science by the 2013-2014 school year. School districts were required to develop a "report card" for each school based on the results, and schools that failed to make "adequate yearly progress" came under increasingly harsh sanctions.

Thus No Child Left Behind turned the evidence of the 1970s successes on its head. Instead of reviving the formula that had produced steady educational progress—a wide network of programs aimed at reducing poverty—the new regime assumed poverty was not the problem at all. Instead, the problem was what George W. Bush, on the campaign trail in 1999, famously dubbed "the soft bigotry of low expectations." Poor children, he said, simply weren't being held to "rigorous standards."

This flimsy analysis quickly became the doctrine that would guide pro-corporate education reformers over the next decades. "Poverty is not destiny," declares the Teach For America website

Gary Huck ©2013

today. "We must help kids growing up in poverty beat the culture of low expectations."

So NCLB willfully ignored poverty. Instead it put the onus for overcoming the achievement gap squarely on teachers while offering them few new tools, resources, or supports to do it—just more pressure. After a school missed its goals on the standardized tests for five years, the district would be obligated to hire a management company to run the school, fire all or most of the staff, or convert the public school to a charter.

NCLB has the power to force these sanctions only onto schools that receive funds from Title I, which is what remains of Johnson's War on Poverty. Those funds are targeted at schools where more than 40 percent of the students come from low-income families. In other words, the big sword is dangled over the heads of students and teachers in working class areas—not rich ones.

In 2006 nearly 30 percent of the nation's schools were not making "adequate yearly progress." By 2012 more than half of all schools were failing to meet NCLB benchmarks.

Critics argue that these results give little guidance to how well, or poorly, students are actually learning. In Massachusetts, for example, only 18 percent of schools posted adequate progress in 2011—compared to Alabama, where 74 percent did. But the results are reversed if you look at the National Assessment of Educational Progress, the apples-to-apples survey conducted by the Department of Education every two years. On almost any dimension Massachusetts sits at the top of state-by-state rankings while Alabama falls to the bottom of the list.

Though the test-heavy approach of NCLB has proven a poor yardstick for measuring student performance, it became a powerful tool for administrators looking to push veteran teachers out of the classroom.

Parents and teachers heavily criticized NCLB. Its exclusive focus on high-stakes tests diverted attention and class time away from other subjects, they argued. Administrators fearful of seeing their schools branded as "failing" were mandating "teaching to the test" at the expense of music, arts, history, and foreign languages. NCLB tests were one-size-fits-all, with little consideration for the needs of special education students or those learning English for the first time. The high stakes also bred shortcuts: cheating scandals emerged in New York, Washington, D.C., and Atlanta, where top administrators sanctioned efforts to doctor student tests to stem a flood of failing grades.

Far from reversing his predecessors' "test-and-punish" prescription for fixing schools, President Obama and his Education Secretary, former Chicago schools CEO Arne Duncan, embraced its central tenets. They introduced Race to the Top, Obama's signature education initiative, in 2009. Race to the Top forced recession-wracked states to compete for $4.3 billion in discretionary federal funds.

To qualify for the money, states must link teacher evaluations to student test scores and expand the use of merit pay. (Traditionally, teacher raises have been based on seniority combined with the achievement of advanced degrees.) In addition, states must remove any cap on the number or percentage of charter schools allowed in the state.

Options for failing schools were narrowed—close, convert to a charter school, or fire the principal and at least 50 percent of the teachers and staff in order to stay open. Race to the Top also created incentives to adopt the "Common Core," a standard curriculum now in use across 45 states, and dramatically expanded official support for charter schools.

Privatizing Public Schools

All this ratcheted-up pressure on public schools boosted the drive to privatize them, which was already underway. In the lead-up to NCLB, Bush made a push for school vouchers, which had also been a Reagan priority. Pitched as offering low-income parents "school choice," a voucher system allows private schools to siphon off a share of public school funding as tuition. Milwaukee became the first city to try it, in 1990. By 2012, a dozen states and D.C. had voucher programs (though some applied only to students with certain disabilities).

In the new millennium, though, the drive for privatization has mostly centered on charters, not vouchers. The push for charter schools exploded under both NCLB and Race to the Top. Today there are more than 6,000 charter schools in the U.S.—almost three times the number of a decade ago (there are about 98,000 public schools).

Charter schools occupy an awkward gray area: publicly funded but privately operated. The idea arose in the late 1980s and early 1990s as a way to help students struggling in big urban districts. The model was student-centered, teacher-run schools that could bypass district bureaucracies and have the flexibility to experiment. Charter schools were often embraced by community organizations, desperate to help failing kids, and some states passed laws to promote them.

But the push for charter schools quickly morphed into something quite different. As the journal *Rethinking Schools* recently explained, "In the past decade, the character of the charter school movement has changed dramatically. It's been transformed from community-based, educator-initiated local efforts designed to provide alternative approaches for a small number of students into nationally funded efforts by foundations, investors, and educational management companies to create a parallel, more privatized school system."

A charter school can be operated by a for-profit chain such as EdisonLearning or by a nonprofit such as Chicago's UNO Charter School Network (even nonprofits, of course, can be quite financially rewarding for their administrators). Nationally, for-profit companies operate 35 percent of charter schools, according to the National Education Policy Center. (Thus far, only nonprofit charters are allowed in Illinois.)

School districts generally allocate about the same amount per pupil to a charter as to a public school, although there may be deductions for services the charter is not required to offer. Many charters also receive much extra money in the form of donations from corporations or wealthy sponsors.

Charters are a bipartisan favorite remedy for what is supposed to ail U.S. schools. Politicians of all stripes are fond of declaring "school choice" as the surefire solution to the racial achievement gap—asking dissatisfied parents to go shopping among schools, rather than striving for equity among them.

According to media portrayals like the NBC series "Education Nation" or the high-profile Hollywood documentary "Waiting for Superman," charters are able to succeed where public schools fail, offering poor children—particularly in big-city black and Latino neighborhoods—a path to college and a ticket to a better life. After Hurricane Katrina, New Orleans replaced nearly all its public schools with charters, and charter schools have exploded in Detroit in the wake of a school district takeover by a state-appointed "emergency manager."

Charter proponents argue that their advantage is innovation—by administrators and teachers alike—something stifled in public schools by government bureaucracy and powerful unions. Teacher unions have been a recurring bogeyman in the charter school debate, and it's no surprise that virtually all charter operators are non-union and working hard to keep it that way.

Don't Believe the Hype

Although charters operate with fewer restrictions and far less oversight than traditional public schools, their track record doesn't measure up to the hype.

According to the most comprehensive evidence available—a 2013 study by a pro-charter research institute at Stanford University—roughly half of charter schools produced outcomes, measured by NCLB-mandated reading and math tests, equivalent to those of traditional public schools. Only 17 percent produced better results, and twice that number did worse.

This is despite the fact that charter schools cherry-pick students (either beforehand or by pushing them out later), avoiding children with special needs, those whose first language isn't English, those with poor grades or attendance, or those with behavior problems. It's a cold, corporate-style risk-management model that leaves public schools with less state funding and fewer resources to educate the more challenging students, since charters have skimmed off the lower-cost students.

High-profile corruption scandals in Florida, Pennsylvania, Illinois, Ohio, and New Jersey—to name just a few recent cases—have also underscored how easy it is to turn charter schools into virtual ATMs for unscrupulous operators looking to line their pockets at the taxpayers' expense.

Chicago's UNO and Los Angeles's Green Dot are among the big operators, and their takeovers are quite explicit—public schools close and new charters open simultaneously, sometimes using the same building. In other places the charters begin as "colocations," taking up part of the space in a public school and eventually squeezing it out.

Dave Vance

Now some states even allow "cyber-charters," where students get a free computer and do "distance learning" from home while the company collects thousands of dollars per student in tuition from the state. As you'd expect, dropout rates are high and test scores are low, but the profits are soaring.

Given their tepid performance, coupled with their vulnerability to fraud and self-dealing, why is the push for charters so strong?

The Corporate Agenda

The answer is that charter schools are just one piece of a much bigger strategy to overhaul how education is delivered. The strategy also involves replacing experienced educators with Teach For America-type recruits; dismantling tenure and teachers' unions; imposing high-stakes testing, standardized curricula, and merit pay; and dreaming up ways to evaluate teachers that make them easier to fire.

For almost two decades, conservative philanthropists who've been served well by capitalism—led by the Waltons, Bill Gates, and Eli Broad—have been pouring billions into this effort. Their motivations are material, political, and ideological.

T.B. Furman

First, education is big business. Corporate execs salivate at the prospect of grabbing a share of the $525 billion of public money spent each year on K-12 schools—a pot nearly as big as the Pentagon budget—and their initial success has only whetted their appetite for more.

Almost two-thirds of that sum—$322 billion—goes to classroom instruction, mainly teacher and support personnel salaries and benefits, so it's no wonder educators have been targeted. Charter operators can make money by paying cheap salaries and offering skimpy benefits, unlike their unionized counterparts.

Even when they don't run an entire school, corporations stand to make money by privatizing various parts of the operation. Consider the $22 billion spent on transportation; $20 billion on food service; $29 billion on support services (such as librarians, multimedia specialists, nurses, speech pathologists); and $10 billion on administration and back-office functions—all of which could be outsourced, and in some cities already is. In Chicago, busing and some janitorial services are privately run. This is not to mention the $56 billion already flowing out to construction contractors, and $18 billion in debt that Wall Streeters would be happy to help school districts "manage"—for hefty fees, of course.

Developing and administering the standardized tests mandated by NCLB has cost states more than a billion dollars a year, according to the General Accounting Office, and charter schools have grown into a nearly $20 billion industry. Sixty years ago corporate interests fused themselves to the Pentagon; today's titans of industry are angling to do the same with education.

Then There's Politics

Second, unions are one of the few non-corporate institutions that can still pull weight for Democrats at election time. While it's no fair fight—unions were outspent by business 15 to 1 in the 2012 election cycle—these movers and shakers still see a reason to blunt unions as a political force. The public sector is 36 percent union, and teachers are its bulwark. Education, training, and library occupations account for 24 percent of all union members. So any education reform strategy that weakens teachers unions is a long-term boon to Republicans. Of course, many Democrats also figure they can get bigger contributions from corporate PACs than from unions.

Third, No Child Left Behind and Race to the Top represented an important political realignment. The Department of Education's new "no excuses" approach to accountability gave conservatives a way to claim the moral high ground on the persistent racial achievement gap on standardized tests, and to paint liberals as defenders of an unacceptable status quo. Some Republicans labeled that achievement gap "the civil rights issue of our generation." Their program for closing it—accountability, not money—lined up perfectly with the conservative agenda.

Fourth, the 1% are uneasy about too much talk of inequality. They'd prefer a scapegoat for the fact that the rich get richer and the poor stay poor—and classroom teachers fit the bill nicely. Blaming teachers for the problems in schools and in society can blunt any possible pressure from the voters for higher taxes on corporations and the rich, the proceeds of which could be used for schools. (Taxes on corporations and the wealthy are now at their lowest point in more than 50 years.)

Through their network of think tanks and advocacy organizations, the billionaires spend lavishly to line up public opinion and politicians to support this ideology.

Democrats Turn on Teachers

The appointment of Arne Duncan as "Reformer-in-Chief" and the rollout of Race to the Top were just two of the steps the

Obama administration took to signal its independence from teachers and their unions. When Obama laid out his initial plans for overhauling education in 2009, he tapped an eighth-grade charter school student to introduce him. Both Obama and Duncan raised ire by praising the mass firing of teachers at Central Falls High School in Rhode Island in 2010.

Everything from the symbols to the sweeping national policy proposals reinforced the about-face that teachers and their unions were experiencing from their own local Democratic politicians.

Perhaps the clearest signal of this shift is Democrats for Education Reform, a political action committee with branches in 12

What's the Story Billionaire Education Reformers Are Peddling?

Whether they're in it for the money or because they think they really care, today's education reformers use a common logic to publicly justify their policies.

It starts from the premise that the key to lifting people out of poverty is education. If only everyone would go to college, they say, they could all pull themselves up by the bootstraps.

This Horatio Alger myth conveniently ignores the fact that our economy is organized with only a thin layer of good, need-a-degree jobs—and a much larger number of bad jobs that mostly require the ability to show up and follow orders.

The best predictor of where a person will fall in the U.S. income hierarchy is where in that hierarchy she or he was born. But those who've hit the jackpot continue to claim that, given the chance, individual strivers can overcome systemic inequality.

Second, these philanthropists are enamored of competition and the private sector—no big surprise, since those systems have worked out so well for them. Surely, they say, the magic of the market can accomplish what bureaucratic mandates have failed to achieve.

Just as we would close a factory that consistently failed to make a profit, we need to close public schools that aren't performing. And just as we make managers responsible for the quality of the widgets they produce, teachers must be responsible for the quality of their students.

That calls for a battery of student test scores to reveal which teachers are failing—and the failures need to ship out: no excuses, no chance to shape up.

Of course, this presupposes that a struggling student's failure can only be caused by a failing teacher—never by an overcrowded classroom, lack of a textbook or counselor, neighborhood violence, lack of motivation, or an empty stomach.

There's also a double standard at work here. The evangelists of education reform don't subject their own kids to the regime they tout for working class youngsters; instead they send them to private schools with plenty of money, small classes, rich curricula, and an emphasis on critical thinking rather than standardized tests. So it's hard believe that even *they* believe the rhetoric they spout.

But sincere or not, the vaunted efficiency of the private sector makes an awfully convenient talking point, deflecting deeper conversations about what it would take to reduce inequality or improve education. More money for schools can't be the answer, because responsible managers make do with less—and besides, higher taxes (on corporations and the rich, anyway) are to be avoided at all costs.

Vouchers and charters go right along with this logic—the market principle will introduce competition among schools, making them more like the private sector. And competition within the workforce can be achieved through merit pay.

These business-minded reformers get away with calling anyone who stands in the way of this agenda—foremost, teachers unions—"entrenched interests preserving the status quo."

In their upside-down world, a hedge fund philanthropist is a bureaucracy-battling hero. And measures like appointed school boards and mayoral control of school districts are strategies to insulate the schools from special interests—teachers. ✿

states. DFER is focused on moving the Democratic Party even further to the right on education. The group lobbies officials and backs candidates in support of more school closures, charters, mayoral control, ending teacher tenure, and more emphasis on testing. Most of DFER's board members work at hedge funds.

Members include Los Angeles Mayor Antonio Villaraigosa, a former union organizer with the L.A. teachers who pulled away from his labor roots to become one of the corporate education agenda's most vocal proponents. In a 2010 editorial, he called teacher unions an "unwavering roadblock to reform." A strong backer of school privatization, he filed an amicus brief in a suit that tied teacher evaluations to student test scores.

Former Newark Mayor Cory Booker, now a U.S. senator, has called teacher tenure "poisonous," saying Republican Governor Chris Christie's sweeping attack on tenure didn't go far enough. Denver Mayor (now Colorado governor) John Hickenlooper backed a Colorado law to weaken tenure and mandate that half of evaluations be based on student test scores. Massachusetts Governor Deval Patrick supported 2012 legislation spearheaded by Stand for Children (and agreed to by the state teachers union) that gutted seniority rights for teachers.

Villaraigosa and Booker figured prominently in the 2012 Democratic National Convention, which took place just days before the CTU walkout. As if to emphasize the administration's take on education reform, the convention's first day featured a screening of the anti-union film "Won't Back Down," sponsored by DFER.

But no one has come to embody the Democratic attack on teachers as much as Rahm Emanuel, Obama's chief of staff for two years before resigning to run for mayor of Chicago. As a candidate, he made weakening the teachers union a main plank of his platform, and it was his anti-student policies that pushed CTU into a strike.

Tenets of Corporate-Style Reform

Attacking Tenure. Tenure in the K-12 system is far less robust than the system of the same name in higher education. It just means due process before a teacher can be fired—what's known in most union workplaces as "just cause." Ordinarily, probationary teachers become eligible for tenure after three or four years in a district.

Nonetheless, the advocacy group Stand for Children has led the charge against teacher tenure in many states, with legislative and ballot measures stressing the easy-to-message theme that performance should trump seniority when it comes to firing and laying off teachers.

Attacking Unions. Attacking teachers unions is an obvious corollary of the bad-teacher dogma, since unions are seen as the defenders of bad teachers.

State legislative attacks continue to roll back teachers' collective bargaining rights. In 2011 alone, Wisconsin, Idaho, and Indiana limited teachers to bargaining over compensation only; Michigan and Nevada created "emergency" loopholes to let states overrule or forcibly reopen contracts; Tennessee and Oklahoma withdrew teachers' bargaining rights altogether. According to the

National Education Association's latest figures, only 34 states and D.C. grant teachers the legal right to bargain. Most prohibit them from striking.

The truth is that Massachusetts, New Jersey, and Connecticut, where teachers are highly unionized and salaries are well above the national average, are the states that consistently get the best test scores. Teachers unions are good for education.

Why? First, the better salaries and benefits bargained by unions encourage teachers to stick around, and a more experienced teacher is a better teacher. In low-pay charters, the turnover is appalling. "If everyone leaves at year two," said CTU Financial Secretary Kristine Mayle, "kids always have lousy teachers."

Policy Pushers

The policy-advocacy group **Stand for Children**—or as some teacher activists call it, "Stand on Children"—has been around since 1999, though it was more benign in its early years. Its public face is co-founder Jonah Edelman. Stand for Children lobbies and supports candidates for office at the state and local levels, pushing mostly for higher-stakes, test-based teacher evaluations. The group claims legislative victories in nine states; one of these was Illinois's Senate Bill 7 in 2011 (see Chapter 7), the law that was supposed to make CTU's strike impossible.

Michelle Rhee founded **Students First** in 2010 after she stepped down as schools chancellor for Washington, D.C. Like Stand for Children, the group is big on attacking tenure and basing teacher evaluations on test scores.

The **American Legislative Exchange Council** is a network of conservative state legislators (mostly Republicans) and corporate lobbyists who craft model bills to advance "free-market enterprise, limited government, and federalism" across a wide range of topics. ALEC claims it manages to enact about 200 of these bills as state laws each year. The group operated quietly for decades, but has gained notoriety in the last few years as activists and journalists have outed its involvement in controversial laws like "Stand Your Ground" and Wisconsin's attack on collective bargaining. It's been especially aggressive in pushing "parent trigger" laws.

If bad teachers are the problem, the solution is simple: replace them. **Teach For America**, founded in 1990, recruits fresh-faced college graduates for a five-week crash course in teaching, then a two-year stint in classrooms in poor schools.

The program started as a way to fill teacher shortages in high-need schools, but has morphed into a de facto hiring hall for school districts and charter networks, charging thousands of dollars for each placement (regardless of whether the teacher finishes out the school year).

Teach For America's approach comes straight out of the lean-management handbook: experience is a liability rather than an asset. "We need people who can think out of the box," Teach For America's backers say, assuming that good teaching requires no special skills—just smarts and enthusiasm. The new teachers are also conveniently cheap replacements for experienced union teachers, even when the placement fees are factored in. In addition to earning the lower salary of a new hire, they don't remain long enough to collect a pension or receive expensive retiree health insurance.

TFA has sent 32,000 teachers into the schools. Most of these young people, well-intentioned but ill-equipped to handle the challenging realities of the job, chalk up a resume credential and move on quickly to another career. The immediate net impact is to make a growing share of teachers temporaries, rather than career professionals.

But TFA has an outsized impact on education policy—far beyond the number of teaching positions it's filled. While three-quarters of its recruits leave the classroom within five years, they typically remain part of the powerful TFA alumni network, pushing its agenda and ensuring the group remains a political powerhouse. From this pool, TFA grooms and channels its favorites into congressional offices, superintendent posts (with training from a personal executive coach), and charter school and nonprofit gigs. Its political spinoff, Leadership for Educational Equality, boosts TFA alums' campaigns for elected offices, too.

The hundreds of millions of dollars that have flowed into TFA's coffers come not only from corporations and funders like the Walton Foundation but also from the Department of Education itself. ✿

A point/counterpoint in the satirical newspaper *The Onion* summed it up perfectly, contrasting a fictional Teach For America-type alum's perspective—"My Year Volunteering as a Teacher Helped Educate a New Generation of Underprivileged Kids"—with a fictional elementary schooler's point of view: "Can We Please, Just Once, Have a Real Teacher?"

Second, unions bargain for other conditions that help teachers teach, such as breaks and preparation time and smaller class sizes. If allowed by law, they can also bargain for resources such

Sarah Jane Rhee, loveandstrugglephotos.com

as libraries, laboratories, nurses, counselors, and social workers.

Third, a union teacher has protection to speak up to the principal and higher authorities about conditions that are bad for kids, such as safety issues or oversized classes, and to resist the latest fad curriculum or silly rules. This includes resisting standardized tests.

Standardized Tests. Standardization is a linchpin in the ideology of corporate education reformers. The performance of both whole schools and individual teachers, according to them, should be measured by performance on standardized tests.

But despite hundreds of millions of dollars spent on research and development, the tests are inconsistent and their results are suspect: the same teacher is rated effective one year and ineffective the next. Study after study shows outcomes are more closely tied to students' socioeconomic status than to anything under the teacher's control. And because the tests are scored to produce a normal distribution of results, someone is always going to be failing.

Teachers also dislike the tests because they steal valuable time. Some Chicago students take as many as 30 standardized tests each year.

Nonetheless, test scores provide statistics reformers can use to beat up on teachers whenever the politics demand it.

Standardized Curriculum. Curriculum is being standardized nationwide through the heavily Gates Foundation-funded "Common Core State Standards Initiative," which lays out what students should know and do at each grade level.

A common curriculum eases the way for standardized tests to become ever more homogenous across states and school districts and also fits with the factory ethos that quality equals precision and uniformity—each product the same size and shape. Teachers have been skeptical about the Common Core because of its ready association with testing and the pressure to bend all lesson plans around it. Many also believe it impedes creativity and makes it difficult to make lessons relevant for their students.

Of course, most states already had standards before Common Core, so teachers suspect that the push for national standards comes from test makers and textbook publishers eager to sell rewritten books and tests. In Los Angeles, for instance, the district distributed $800 iPads containing preset lesson plans and assignments, linked to the Common Core, from Pearson, a top education software company.

Evaluations: VAM or Sham? "All the part about evaluations being used to help people improve their teaching has dropped out of the equation," said Gene Bruskin, who works with the national Teachers union. "Now it's just about how to punish people."

Teachers have traditionally been evaluated, often by their principal, through observation of their classroom work. But Race to the Top favors districts that use student test scores, often through "value-added models" (VAMs) that rate teachers by measuring students' improvement, or lack thereof, over time.

Besides the fact that judging teachers based on their students' progress doesn't factor in all the outside influences in students' lives, CTU leaders and other teacher unionists say the value-added model leads to inconsistent, inaccurate ratings. In Chicago, says Kristine Mayle, teachers aren't even allowed to know what the value-added algorithm is—it's patented.

New York City's teachers union lost a two-year battle with the city's Department of Education in 2012 when the city publicly released controversial teacher "data reports," rating elementary and middle school teachers on a 0 to 100 scale by their students' performance on state standardized tests. New York tabloids wasted no time, screaming from the headlines about the "city's worst teachers."

The scores were "flawed and humiliating," elementary school teacher Sarah Levine wrote for *Labor Notes* after her scores and those of more than 18,000 others were published. Her own report was full of errors—half the students were left off the roster;

Strings Attached

As labor folksinger Utah Phillips used to say, "A Robin Hood bandit gives away privately what he steals publicly, whereas a philanthropist... Well, you figure it out." Like the robber barons of yore, today's corporate tycoons are big on philanthropy—and all the groups pushing education reform are big beneficiaries of their largesse.

The big three funders, the ones education historian Diane Ravitch calls the "Billionaire Boys' Club," are the Broad, Gates, and Walton foundations. Since profit, not teaching, is these patrons' strong suit, it's no surprise they all pitch their school solutions in business-speak: competition, innovation, entrepreneurship.

The **Eli and Edythe Broad Foundation**, assets $2.1 billion, focuses on "entrepreneurship for the public good in education, science and the arts." That means charter schools and putting business execs in charge of school districts. They do their work through grants (sample grantees: Teach For America (TFA), charter operator Green Dot, the anti-teacher-union movie "Waiting for Superman") and an academy for superintendents and principals (sample alumnus: Jean-Claude Brizard, Chicago Public Schools CEO 2011-12).

Walmart founders Sam and Helen Walton were the money behind the **Walton Family Foundation**, assets $1.7 billion. Education reform is one of its three focus areas. "Our core strategy is to infuse competitive pressure into America's K-12 education system," the foundation claims, "by increasing the quantity and quality of school choices available to parents, especially in low-income communities." That translates into pushing charters and vouchers, school closures, and teacher evaluation/compensation changes, and subsidizing TFA.

The **Bill and Melinda Gates Foundation**, assets $38.3 billion, has an outsized influence because it is so super-rich. The Gateses spent years pushing to break up bigger schools into smaller ones; eventually they admitted that wasn't working, and jumped onto a new bandwagon: merit pay, turnarounds, and lots of testing. The foundation is big on standardization— it was the driving funder behind the national Common Core standards—and, big surprise, technology in the classroom. ✿

her two best readers were omitted because they'd taken the test a couple days late—and gave an absurdly wide margin of error (she was told her score could be anywhere from 15 to 90, out of 100).

But more than that, Levine said, the value-added measures can put teachers' livelihoods in conflict with students' needs. In her school, the test produced an impetus to work only with students officially on her roster, to improve their scores—though she was team-teaching other students as well. The incentive is to teach to the tests.

Merit Pay. Closely paired with testing, evaluations, and attacks on tenure is the push for merit pay—linking teachers' compensation to the tests and evaluations, supposedly to create an incentive for them to improve—though the research shows it just doesn't work. One Nashville study offered one group of teachers $15,000 each if they could raise their test scores in three years. A control group was offered no such reward, yet those teachers did just as well—because, of course, both groups were teaching the best they knew how, with the resources available to them. "It's not as if teachers are sitting on their best lessons waiting for a bonus," as education historian Diane Ravitch put it.

Parent Trigger Laws. The secretive and conservative bill-writing group American Legislative Exchange Council (ALEC) has been a big driver of "parent trigger" laws. So has a nonprofit called Parent Revolution. The Hollywood movie "Won't Back Down" (which flopped, mercifully) was an advertisement for parent trigger.

In 2010 California was the first state to pass a law allowing parents to petition to change their public school to a charter, or make other changes such as forcing out a principal. It was followed by Connecticut, Indiana, Louisiana, Mississippi, Ohio, and Texas.

The charter trigger has only been tried a few times, all in California so far, with heavy involvement by Parent Revolution. Though "parent unions" form to run the petition drives, paid staffers from Parent Revolution do a lot of the actual signature-gathering. The first couple of efforts left parents feeling tricked and pressured (thus the nickname "parent tricker"). Many tried to revoke their signatures, resulting in court battles until a judge ruled the signatures irrevocable. The first two charter schools to be "triggered" under these new laws opened in California in 2013.

Buying the Votes

How do the corporate-friendly reformers get their way? Their preferred setup is mayoral control of the schools, but if an elected school board exists, money can be applied to get their candidates in. For instance, Students First, the Broad Foundation, the California Charter Schools Association, and New York Mayor Michael Bloomberg dropped nearly $4 million on candidates for three Los Angeles school board seats in 2013. Despite all this cash, underdogs managed to win two out of three races. But more often, the money prevails.

Just a few months after the CORE slate won leadership of CTU in 2010, Stand for Children swooped into Illinois to drum up over a half-million dollars in last-minute donations to nine state legislative campaigns. Six of its candidates won, helping set the stage for passage of anti-union Senate Bill 7. The group again ponied up close to a half-million dollars for 2012 races, and swept the field: all 14 of its candidates won.

Another popular method for imposing the corporate agenda on cash-strapped cities is old-fashioned bribery. As chancellor of D.C. schools, Michelle Rhee lined up $64.5 million from the Broad, Walton, and other foundations to finance teacher bonuses—with strings attached that gave her tighter control over evaluating and firing teachers. The union took the deal. When the foundations' three-year commitment ended, much of the funding dried up—leaving individual schools on the hook to pay for the bonus program.

Money talks. Facebook founder Mark Zuckerberg gave a whopping $100 million to Newark schools in 2010 to be spent on merit pay. (Most of that is still sitting untouched—in the last cycle, only 5 percent of teachers got the bonus.) A $430,000 Broad Foundation grant to New Jersey for public education came with the stipulation that Republican Governor Chris Christie remain in office. And a series of contributions from the Wasserman Foundation to the Los Angeles school district have come earmarked—for instance, $1 million in 2011 was tied to the "Public School Choice" (charter) program.

Unions Offer Concessions, Lie Low

At the national level, both the American Federation of Teachers (AFT) and the National Education Association (NEA) were wholly unprepared for the tidal wave of criticism leveled against teachers over the past decade.

In the face of the storm, the two unions tacked between harsh criticism of the education reformers and tentative embrace. The AFT—of which the Chicago Teachers Union is Local 1—took the more conciliatory approach, asking only for a seat at the reform table and pushing its locals to take concessions in the name of teacher-management partnership. At its 2010 convention, Bill Gates was keynote speaker.

The larger NEA took a tougher stance at first, filing a lawsuit against the Department of Education to try to block implementation of No Child Left Behind, but this legalistic approach didn't have a member-organizing component. There was no real strategy to succeed.

The two unions' trajectories paralleled those of most public sector unions, which historically have been wary of voters and eager to stay out of the public eye. In recent decades leaders have tried to win gains for members through relationships with politicians, especially Democrats, rather than by allying with the public or mobilizing members. They have chosen to lie low and hope that public employees' wages and benefits did not become topics of public discussion, especially after companies in the private sector began gutting unions there in the 1980s.

Thus public employee unions, for much of their history, did not lead the charge for improving public services, and teachers unions didn't take on a fight to overhaul the schools, for fear of stirring up criticism of their members. Leaders' default position became preemptive compromise.

Teachers began accepting major concessions, often at the prodding of national AFT officials. In Pittsburgh, for instance, the local took a deal in 2010 that introduced merit pay for new hires and raised the number of years to gain tenure. When Baltimore members rejected a merit-based contract in 2010, AFT top brass swooped in to pressure members to change their votes. After the deal went through on a second vote, an unprecedented majority of Baltimore teachers received unsatisfactory mid-year evaluations in what teachers say was a deliberate attempt to avoid merit raises. Since then teachers in Newark and New Haven have also settled for merit pay, with the AFT's endorsement.

St. Louis teachers' 2010 deal diluted tenure, empowering principals to deem even senior teachers "ineffective" and put them on a fast track to firing. The St. Louis Plan has booted 100 teachers, but AFT President Randi Weingarten still touts it as a model.

Even in the union stronghold of Massachusetts—where student test scores are the highest in the country—the NEA affiliate lost its nerve when Stand for Children showed up with millions of corporate dollars to attack tenure. The group's paid signature-gatherers quickly qualified a referendum for the 2012 ballot to make teacher evaluations trump seniority. Instead of mounting a defense, the president of the Massachusetts Teachers Association opted for closed-door negotiations, leading to a concessionary compromise where Stand for Children withdrew the measure.

Unfortunately, preemptive concessions seemed like common sense to battered teachers. "I'm glad we gave in; if we hadn't, we would have been beaten much worse," one Massachusetts teacher explained.

Looking at the strength of the forces arrayed against teachers, it's not hard to see how a person could feel that way. But it was just a few months later that CTU struck—drawing the eyes of the country, and transforming what seemed possible for teachers anywhere.

CTU

Timeline

1995

The Illinois legislature passes a bill that replaces the elected Chicago school board with a board appointed by the mayor. The teachers union is stripped of its legal right to bargain over class size, school schedules, and charter schools.

2004

Mayor Richard M. Daley and Schools CEO Arne Duncan introduce the Renaissance 2010 initiative to close "failing" schools and open charters.

Teacher activists who will later found CORE, together with community organizations, begin organizing against school closings.

2007

Soon-to-be CORE members Jackson Potter and Al Ramirez team up to produce "Renaissance 2010: On the Front Lines," an hour-long documentary that examines the effort to bust the teachers union and corporatize education.

Spring 2008

CORE is founded.

Fall 2008

Grassroots Education Movement (GEM) coalition is formalized, including CORE, Parents United for Responsible Education, Designs for Change, Blocks Together, Kenwood Oakland Community Organization, Pilsen Alliance, Teachers for Social Justice, and others.

Winter 2008-9

Twenty-two school closings are announced (eventually reduced to 16 closed/turned around).

CPS CEO Arne Duncan is appointed Secretary of Education in the Obama Administration.

CORE holds a summit; 500 teachers, parents, and students attend to fight school closings.

Fall 2009	CORE runs candidates for the CPS Pension Board. Jay Rehak and Lois Ashford both win spots.
Winter 2009-10	Fourteen school closings are announced (eventually reduced to eight closed/turned around). CORE activists attend every hearing.
	CORE holds another summit and announces a slate for union leadership; 400 people attend.
Spring 2010	CORE organizes the Save Our Schools rally, and successfully pressures incumbent CTU leaders to endorse it. Five thousand attend.
	CORE slate is elected to head CTU.
Summer 2010	CTU rejects the district's proposal to open the contract and forego a 4 percent raise. Layoffs are announced.
Fall 2010	CTU's new leaders begin their first school year in office. They start an Organizing Department and launch a program to recruit, train, and activate delegates and district supervisors.
	Mayor Daley announces he will not run again. Rahm Emanuel throws his hat in the ring.
	A judge rules that 749 of the 1,300 summer layoffs were improper because they violated seniority rules. The district appeals.
	CPS CEO Ron Huberman resigns; interim CEO Terry Mazany is appointed.
Winter 2010-11	CTU leaders fight the legislature over pensions, fending off big cuts.
	Eight schools are announced to be closed/turned around/consolidated/phased out (six eventually pushed through).
Winter 2010-11	Rahm Emanuel is elected mayor.
	CTU activists join the occupation of a

Cadillac dealership to protest misuse of TIF funds.

Spring 2011   Emanuel selects Jean-Claude Brizard as CPS CEO.

Senate Bill 7 passes, requiring at least a quarter of a teacher's evaluation to be based on student performance, giving the school district the unilateral right to lengthen the school day, and requiring a vote of 75 percent of CTU members to authorize a strike.

Emanuel takes office and makes the longer school day his first education issue.

Summer 2011   Stand up Chicago and CTU protest at a meeting of corporate CFOs at a downtown hotel, bringing attention to the misuse of TIF funds that could go to schools; 3,000 people attend.

CORE organizes a conference for teacher activists from 15 states.

The district asks CTU to agree to a longer school day with a 2 percent raise, without a plan to hire more teaching staff. CTU rejects the offer, and campaigns for a "better school day" instead.

Fall 2011   CTU begins its contract campaign. This includes holding big meetings to develop bargaining demands, recruiting and training a Contract Action Committee in each school, and on-the-job activities to gauge support.

Emanuel and CPS go around the union, getting some individual schools to waive the contract and agree to the longer school day. A judge later rules the action a violation of teachers' collective bargaining rights.

As part of the Stand Up Chicago coalition, CTU protests the Mortgage Bankers Association.

Winter 2011-12   Seventeen schools are announced for closing/ turnaround/phase-out, plus six co-locations with charters (all 23 actions eventually pushed through).

A CTU teach-in brings parents, teachers, and community organizations together to strategize how to fight against school closings announced December 1.

Parents "mic check" the school board, which flees into executive session.

Rallies and vigils against school closings. Parents occupy Piccolo School.

CTU publishes the report *The Schools Chicago's Students Deserve.*

Delegates start conducting impromptu strike votes at their schools.

Spring 2012   CTU wins 21,000 yes votes—more than 80 percent of members—in a practice strike vote.

7,000 CTU members fill an auditorium for a huge rally, overflowing into the streets. The crowd marches through downtown.

CTU wins 24,000 yes votes—90 percent of members—in its actual strike vote.

Summer 2012   CTU's contract expires.

The district and union both reject an arbitrator's report, setting the stage for a strike.

CTU and the district agree to a longer school day compromise, with the day lengthened and more teachers hired to fill the gaps.

The union holds informational pickets at schools that open early. Strike captains and coordinators are trained.

September 10-18   CTU teachers strike for nine days, with near-unanimous participation in picket lines and huge downtown rallies. Strikers enjoy an outpouring of community support; polls show majorities of voters and parents back them.

After two days spent reading a tentative agreement, members tell delegates to end the strike.

Fall 2012   Members vote by 79 percent to ratify the contract.

CPS CEO Brizard resigns, replaced by Cleveland school district CEO Barbara Byrd-Bennett.

CTU publishes another report, *The Black and White of Education in Chicago's Public Schools*, showing the negative impacts of district policies on black, Latino, and low-income students.

Working with Teachers for Social Justice and Action Now, teachers sit in at City Hall, calling for a moratorium on school closings. Ten are arrested.

Spring 2013   CTU holds a downtown rally against school closings.

CTU holds a three-day march for education justice through Chicago's South and West Sides to downtown.

After announcing 54 elementary schools to be closed, the district goes ahead with 47 school closings before the 2013-14 school year.

CORE slate is reelected.

Summer 2013   CORE hosts another Social Justice Unionism conference. Teachers from across the country attend.

Fall 2013   CTU launches its "Let Us Teach!" campaign against over-testing.

Glossary

Albany Park Neighborhood Council—a Northwest Side community group allied with CTU.

American Federation of Teachers (AFT)—CTU's parent union. The AFT is one of two national teachers unions; the other is NEA.

Caucus of Rank-and-File Educators (CORE)—the member caucus formed in 2008 to fight school closings, which won leadership of CTU in 2010.

Charter school—a school that receives public funds but is operated by a private organization, for-profit or nonprofit.

Chicago Public Schools (CPS)—the school district.

Chicago Teachers Union (CTU)—AFT Local 1. Its members include teachers, paraprofessionals, and clinicians.

Clinicians—school nurses, psychologists, speech pathologists, counselors, social workers, occupational therapists, physical therapists. They are CTU members.

Community Board—the coalition of community groups established by CTU in 2010. Most of its members had been part of a similar group called GEM that worked with CORE before the caucus won leadership of the union. The Community Board formally renamed itself GEM again in 2012.

Contract Action Committee—the union's member-to-member network in each school, used to communicate and mobilize during the contract campaign before the strike.

Delegate—union steward and elected representative from a school to the union's House of Delegates. Most schools have one, larger schools have more; some delegates are elected by citywide groupings of members. CTU delegates also head up their schools' Professional Problems Committees.

District supervisor—an appointed CTU position, responsible for contact with delegates in nine to 23 schools.

Grassroots Education Movement (GEM)—the coalition of community groups working with CORE, and later CTU.

House of Delegates—CTU's 800-delegate body, which meets monthly.

Kenwood Oakland Community Organization (KOCO)—a South Side community group closely involved with CTU in fighting for better public schools.

Local School Council (LSC)—a body in each Chicago school composed of two teacher reps, six parents, two community reps, and the principal, plus a student rep in high schools. One non-teacher school worker was added to the LSCs in 2011. They vote on the school's budget and can hire and fire the principal.

Mandatory subjects of bargaining—topics the school board is required to bargain over, such as wages. (Compare to permissive subjects.)

Mayoral control—when a school board is appointed by the mayor rather than elected by voters. New York and Chicago have mayor-run districts.

National Education Association (NEA)—the larger of two national teachers unions. CTU is affiliated to the other one, AFT.

Network—CPS's term for a geographical region of the city.

Paraprofessionals and School-Related Personnel (PSRP)—such as clerks, teaching assistants, interpreters, social service assistants, and hearing and vision screeners. They are CTU members.

Permissive subjects of bargaining—topics the school board is not required to bargain over, such as class size. (Compare to mandatory subjects.)

ProActive Chicago Teachers (PACT)—a reform caucus that ran CTU from 2001 to 2004.

Professional Problems Committee (PPC)—an elected committee of three to five members in each school, mandated by the contract and led by the delegate, which meets monthly with the principal to resolve issues before they become grievances.

Renaissance 2010—a 2004 plan by Mayor Richard M. Daley and schools CEO Arne Duncan to close "failing schools" and open charters to compete with traditional public schools.

Substance News—a print and online journal that reports on Chicago schools and national education issues.

Tax Increment Financing (TIF)—a pot of money pooled from property tax increases that the mayor has discretion to use for development projects in "blighted" areas of the city.

Teachers for Social Justice (TSJ)—an organization of Chicago educators with an activist, anti-racist perspective. They work to improve education inside and outside the classroom.

Teach For America—an organization that recruits and trains college graduates for two-year stints in poor schools. Its philosophy is that experienced teachers are part of the problem.

Turnaround—a district plan to rejuvenate a school by firing the whole staff; members may reapply for their jobs.

United Progressive Caucus (UPC)—the caucus that led CTU for 37 of the years 1970-2010.

Acknowledgments

This book—like the organizing it chronicles—was a group effort. Without dozens of people generously sharing their time and knowledge and tolerating our incessant questions, we could not have written it.

First, the book rests on a foundation of meticulous reporting by former Labor Notes staffers Paul Abowd, Theresa Moran, and Howard Ryan, who chronicled the Chicago teachers' story before and during the strike. We've drawn on their published and unpublished work.

People we talked to for the book are Steven Ashby, Xian Barrett, Raul Botello, Kimberly Bowsky, Jitu Brown, Michael Brunson, Gene Bruskin, Carol Caref, Anne Carlson, Jim Cavallero, Sarah Chambers, Emily Gann, Alix Gonzalez Guevara, Norine Gutekanst, Rico Gutstein, Alex Han, Adam Heenan, David Hernandez, Brandon Johnson, Jen Johnson, Katelyn Johnson, Wendy Katten, Bill Lamme, Karen Lewis, Matthew Luskin, Kristine Mayle, Veronica McDaniel, Tim Meegan, Margo Murray, Andrea Parker, Debby Pope, Jackson Potter, Al Ramirez, Nate Rasmussen, Charlotte Sanders, Jesse Sharkey, Kenzo Shibata, Jerry Skinner, Phyllis Trottman, Tammie Vinson, Latoya Walls, and Latrice Watkins. Thanks so much to each of you.

Special thanks are due to Jennifer Berkshire, Carol Caref, Norine Gutekanst, Karen Lewis, Matthew Luskin, Kristine Mayle, Debby Pope, and Jackson Potter, who gave perceptive feedback on the manuscript. The book is stronger for their insights.

Many sources enriched our understanding—too many to credit here—but we owe a particular debt to Kenzo Shibata and the other contributors to the CORE Teachers blog; George Schmidt and the other contributors to *Substance News*; Steven Ashby, who shared a paper presented at a United Association for Labor Education conference; and the work of Diane Ravitch. Any errors, of course, are ours alone.

Finally, we're grateful to intrepid editor/proofreader Hanna Metzger; to Stacey Luce, who designed the cover; to Sarah Jane Rhee (loveandstrugglephotos.com), who shared her wonderful photographs, and to Jen Johnson, who wrote the perfect foreword. Our own Jenny Brown designed and laid out the book's insides.